Other titles in this series:

Pensions Simplified

A complete guide to the current pensions system. The book includes a full description of current entitlements under the various types of pension scheme available, both from the State and privately, and gives detailed advice on how to set up a tax-efficient scheme to protect your own future. Areas covered include: • how to choose a pension, set it up and care for it • taking account of the tax implications • retirement planning • what choices are offered at retirement • transfers and opt-outs • dealing with divorce and mortgages • death before and after retirement.

Inheritance Tax Simplified

This book is a detailed practical guide to inheritance tax and estate planning. Packed with tips, advice and examples, the book shows how to plan to minimise inheritance taxes, whilst successfully planning for your estate, wills and trusts. Areas covered include • everything you need to know about inheritance tax • estate planning • choices and money-saving options • how not to lose your house whilst staying in it • preserving and protecting your estate assets • how wills work and why you should have one • how to make substantial savings at very low cost • and a host of other relevant information.

Succession Planning Simplified

Succession planning – planning for the future ownership and management of a business after the death or departure of a key executive – is often left until the last minute – or not done at all. However, the benefits of advance planning can be enormous, not only in protecting the value of the business for the owner's heirs and successors, but also in ensuring a viable future for staff and employees. *Succession Planning Simplified* is a practical guide to the whole area, including a review of legal and taxation implications of the various alternative types of succession plan, and a thorough explanation of the planning methodology involved.

Taxation Simplified

A concise guide to all the basic forms of taxation in the UK. Now in its 105th edition, this is the longest established tax guide of its kind – including practical down-to-earth descriptions of all the principal areas and methods of taxation, and packed with tips and advice for reducing or avoiding tax. Areas covered include: • income tax • corporation tax • capital allowances • capital gains tax • inheritance tax • value added tax • council tax • self-assessment.

**For further information on any of these books visit www.mb2000.com
or telephone Management Books 2000 on 01285 771441**

The complete list of books in the Simplified series is:

Business Protection Simplified

Inheritance Tax Simplified

Pensions Simplified

School and University Fees Simplified

Succession Planning Simplified

Taxation Simplified

Tax-Efficient Investments Simplified

Tax-Efficient Wills Simplified

For further information on any of these titles,
or for a complete list of Management Books 2000 titles
visit our web-site, **www.mb2000.com**

TAX-EFFICIENT
INVESTMENTS
SIMPLIFIED

Tony Granger

2000

This edition first published in 2010 by Management Books 2000 Ltd
Forge House, Limes Road
Kemble, Cirencester
Gloucestershire, GL7 6AD, UK
Tel: 0044 (0) 1285 771441
Fax: 0044 (0) 1285 771055
E-mail: info@mb2000.com
Web: www.mb2000.com

British Library Cataloguing in Publication Data is available

ISBN 97818525259726658

About the Author

Tony Granger has been advising investors and training investment advisers for more than 25 years. He is responsible for many innovations in the financial planning field to make complicated financial planning concepts easy to understand for both lay and professional readers.

He is the is the author of many publications and books, including *How to Finance Your Retirement* (Random House/Century), *Wealth Strategies for Your Business* (Random House/Century), *EIS and VCT Investors' Guide* (30 Day Publishing), *Independent Financial Advice and Fee-Based Financial Planning* and the *Retirement Planning Workstation* (30 Day Publishing) which includes booklets on 'Annuities', 'Pensions' and 'Estate Planning', *School and University Fees Simplified* (Management Books 2000), *Inheritance Tax Simplified* (Management Books 2000), *Business Protection Simplified* (Management Books 2000) and *Succession Planning Simplified* (Management Books 2000).

Tony is a member of the Institute of Financial Planning and holds the CFP, the certified financial planner certificate, as well as degrees in law and commerce. He is a past president of the Institute of Life and Pensions Advisers (Financial Planning Institute) of South Africa, and a member of the Personal Finance Society (PFS). He lectures regularly to accountants and solicitors, as well as independent financial advisers on a wide range of issues.

Tax-Efficient Investments Simplified is aimed at consumers and financial advisers alike, and is most topical as people decide on their investment planning strategies in the face of higher taxation; trustees make decisions on how trust monies should be invested, following the recent increase in trust tax rates; and business owners seek the best avenues to invest company, Partnership/ LLP and sole trader money. Being more efficient with your investments can increase the net return to you and may even reduce the costs of making investments that would otherwise be subject to tax. Knowing what your investment universe is and what investments and strategies are available to you, together with your attitude to investment risk, could be deciding factors in deciding on which investments to make and when to make them.

Acknowledgements

Nick Dale-Harris, the Publisher at Management Books 2000, continues to support my written financial planning initiatives and book writing, and his dynamic approach and guidance in bringing together easily understandable concepts for the reading public is not to be under – estimated. My thanks to him for his superb organisation in this respect.

Octopus Investments is a leading investment management service, responsible for many new innovative tax-efficient products. Their assistance as sponsor in bringing this book to market is appreciated, as this will ensure the widest possible distribution, supported by seminars for professional intermediaries and the wider public. My special thanks to them.

To the many product providers and technical advisers in the financial services industry, this book on Tax-Efficient Investments Simplified can also be said to be a distillation of your ideas and works, and I am grateful for your support.

Contents

Forewords

I am pleased to commend this book on tax-efficient investments. This book is being launched in Financial Planning Week, and will serve to highlight the importance of the need for proper financial planning when making investments. Recent times have seen a sharp increase in taxation for both income tax and capital gains tax, and the freezing of some personal allowances such as the inheritance tax nil rate band and reduction of other allowances, such as the personal allowance for earnings over £100,000, and the maximum contributions for pension funding. Making the most of what is allowed by legislation is therefore of prime importance, as is the need to plan investments for the best returns and growth possibilities. It is extremely important to seek the advice of a Certified Financial Planner professional to ensure that planning needs are taken care of.

Nick Cann
CEO of the Institute of Financial Planning

Tax mitigation is an essential part of an individual's long-term financial planning, helping to preserve cash and assets in the face of income tax, capital gains tax and inheritance tax (IHT). With tax rises and reductions to tax relief on pensions, particularly for higher earners, more investors will be turning to tax-efficient products for capital protection and growth.

At Octopus, we've always been focused on meeting customers' needs. We've listened to customers and designed tax-efficient solutions based around these. We've produced a range of tax-efficient products to meet different customer needs, each of which is simple and flexible, and can reduce an investor's tax burden, whatever their appetite for risk.

Tax mitigation is relatively complex and, due to shifting legislation, is constantly evolving. We know from our discussions with investors and advisers that they appreciate clear explanations of the issues surrounding tax mitigation, along with solutions that not only deliver but can be easily understood. That's why we are delighted to sponsor *Tax-Efficient Investments – Simplified* by Tony Granger, who is both a financial expert and seasoned author. For anyone interested in tax mitigation, this book is indispensable."

Simon Rogerson
Chief Executive
Octopus Investments

Introduction

Investments! For some a constant source of panic and disappointment, for others, a planned and controlled experience, where their outcomes are measured, and their expectations are met.

Hardly a week goes past without someone saying 'well, you're a financial adviser, what's the best investment for me at this time'? There is no straight answer, the reason being that not only do we invest for different reasons, but everyone has different circumstances and their attitudes to risk and time frames will also vary. This is where the astute financial planner and investment adviser earns his or her spurs. The advice process involves fact-finding your personal details and establishing your objectives and goals, and attitude to risk, before a recommendation can be made. Interestingly enough, the *Trustee Act 2000* lays down a process for considering the suitability of investments, the need for diversification, the size of the investment, the need for balance in respect of income and growth; and the need for regular reviews, amongst other considerations. **Section 4(1)** provides that where exercising a power of investment, a trustee must have regard to the suitability to the trust of the investment, and where appropriate, to the need for diversification of the trust's investments. **Section 4(3)** defines this as standard investment criteria. 'Suitability' includes the type of investment proposed, and to consider its size, the risk of the investment, and the need to produce an appropriate balance between income and capital growth to meet the needs of the trust; as well as ethical considerations. The standard investment criteria are core. Other considerations may also have to be made with regard to diversification, the need for tax planning, asset allocation and other factors.

Section 4(2) requires the trustees to keep investments of the trust under review and to consider whether, in the light of standard investment criteria, they should be varied.

This advice for trustees should also be the same for any investor and their adviser(s), and is the only legislation that gives guidance on what to take into account when making investments.

A number of factors have sharply focussed the minds of investors as to how to get the best out of their investments in respect of growth and return. With a Government desperate to swell its coffers from consumers, we have recently experienced the following:

- Increased taxation for individuals and trusts, with a new top rate of income tax of 50%; and dividends to be taxed at 42.5% for additional rate taxpayers and trusts.
- Capital Gains Tax increased from 18%-28% for higher earners.
- Freezing of the personal allowance (although this will go up by £1,000 from April 2011).

- Loss of the personal allowance for earners over £100,000 in steps to around £112,000.
- Freezing of the Inheritance Tax nil rate band at £325,000.
- Reduction of maximum pension funding to £50,000 per annum – from £255,000 – from April 2011; reduction of the lifetime allowance from £1,8 million to £1.5 million.
- Increase in VAT from 17.5% to 20% from 4.1.2011
- National insurance contributions to rise by 1% from 6.4.2011.
- Child tax credits withdrawn for those earning more than £41,329 from 6.4.2011. Child benefit withdrawn for higher-rate taxpayers from January 2013; Child Trust Funds (CTF's) payments to cease from 1 January 2011.
- National Savings index linked bonds withdrawn (as too popular).

On the bright side, we have recently had an increase in ISA allowances up to £10,200 and Entrepreneur's relief was increased from £2 million to £5 million where gains from selling the business are taxed at 10%. However, these handouts are few and far between, and most people will be adopting wealth preservation measures in their future planning to maximum their income and capital growth from investments.

The main problem is that investments promising higher possible returns are also those where the riskiness of investing into them is higher. Most investors I talk to are happy not to be making money so long as they are not losing capital – however this does mean fixed deposit type investments, usually with returns below inflation.

So what can investors do to increase their returns? This book is brimful of ideas on where to invest, and how to use tax and other strategies to increase your net wealth. It is a primary principle of our law that you can arrange your financial affairs in any legal way to avoid the tax take of the Fiscus. This book is concerned with the legal ways to develop your investment and financial planning. I know that there are tax strategies out there that may reduce your tax – there again they may not – and the HMRC has proved swift to combat any new innovative ways to avoid tax. Fortunately we have many different investment opportunities to consider for your investment planning.

The core focus of the book is divided into three main parts. The first is on tax-free investments; then tax-reducing investments; followed by taxable investments that can be tax-efficient.

Tony Granger
November 2010

Disclaimer

Please do not act on strategies or information unless you have confirmed your proposed actions with a qualified financial or tax adviser, and taken the appropriate advice before acting, as the author, publisher, sponsor, and information providers in this book cannot be responsible for your actions and do not accept liability for them. The information given is based on tax and other legislation as at 1st November 2010, and this may change in the future. As is common, when discussing investments, the value of an investment may go down as well as up, and you may lose your capital.

If you take out loans or mortgages, be sure to service them, or your asset or home could be at risk.

1

Investment Planning

Financial planning with investments

The financial definition of 'investment' is to create more money through the use of capital. This could be the investing of money or capital in order to gain profitable returns, as interest, income, or appreciation in value. In practice though, no precise definition distinguishes between investment and speculation.

Understanding asset allocation

Investors need to understand the different asset classes and investment options as well as the process of investment planning. There is no perfect single investment that will meet the needs of any one client. Most investors should hold a spread of asset classes, and also have money available for emergencies. Asset spreading and asset allocation is the most important decision an investor can make – this is because it affects overall investment performance far more than market timing or making individual investment selections.

If your asset allocation is correct, it can also reduce your risk. This is because different asset classes perform differently under diverse economic conditions. Most investments are correlated in some way. This means that they are affected by economic and financial conditions, such as the movement of interest rates, and inflation. Usually, for example, if interest rates go up, the capital value of gilts goes down. For example, a 0.5% increase in interest rates could reduce the price of a gilt with a 10 year term by 5%. Some investments are said to be uncorrelated – for example, life settlements, where the investment returns are based on the life expectancy of an individual, rather than market performance. However, recent events (the global economic downturn) has shown that this is not always the case, as the buying and selling of these policies were priced according to supply and demand, which affected their pricing.

The need for diversification

Not every investment asset class will always be at the top of the performance tree. One year UK equities may be the best buy, the next year bonds, the next year property, or commodities. This year's star is often next year's dog. It is therefore most important to spread your investments and to diversify them for sustainable returns.

The following Table shows the best performing investments for the past 6 years *(Source Zurich/also Scottish Widows and 7IM.)*

2004	2005	2006	2007	2008	2009
UK Property shares 45.3%	EM Equity 48.8%	UK Property Shares 47.9%	EM Equity 36.2%	Global Govt Bonds 50.7%	EM Equity 64.1%
UK Property 18.3%	Japan Equity 40.8%	European Equity 20.5%	Gold 27.6%	Gold 42.8%	Private Equity 47.6%
Private Equity 15.1%	Private Equity 39.4%	UK Property 18.1%	Commodities 20.6%	Emerg. Mkt Bonds 22.5%	UK Equity 18.3%
EM Equity 14.4%	Commodities 33%	EM Equity 17.9%	European Equity 17.1%	Timber 9.5%	European Equity 12.6%
UK Equity 12.8%	Gold 30.6%	UK Equity 16.8%	Global Govt Bonds 7.6%	Gilts 7.4%	US Equity 14.5%
European Equity 12.6%	Timber 27.4%	Private Equity 13.5%	Cash 5.9%	Cash 6.2%	Gold 14.4%
Index linked 8.5%	Emerg. Mkt Bonds 23.4%	Gold 9.4%	UK Equity 5.3%	Index linked 3.7%	Emerg. Mkt Bonds 13.9%
Corporate Bonds 6.9%	European Equity 22.5%	Cash 4.7%	Index linked 5.3%	Japan Equity -0.6%	Hedge Funds 13.4%
Gilts 6.6%	UK Equity 22%	Hedge Funds 4.3%	Gilts 5.3%	Corporate Bonds -8.5%	Corporate Bonds 12.3%
Hedge Funds 6%	UK Property shares 21.2%	Timber 3.7%	Emerg. Mkt Bonds 4.9%	Commodities -11.8%	Commodities 12.6%
Japan Equity 4.9%	UK Property 19.1%	Index linked 2.9%	Hedge Funds 4.5%	US Equity -14.5%	UK Property Shares 11.8%
Cash 4.6%	US Equity 16.9%	US Equity 1.7%	US Equity 4.1%	UK Property -22.5%	Index linked 6.4%
Commodities 4.2%	Corporate Bonds 12.2%	Corporate Bonds 0.8%	Timber 2.6%	Hedge Funds -22.8%	UK Property 2.2%
Emerg. Mkt Bonds 4%	Index linked 9%	Gilts 0.7%	Corporate Bonds 0.2%	European Equity -28%	Cash 1.5%
US Equity 3.2%	Gilts 7.9%	Emerg. Mkt Bonds -3.5%	UK Property -1.8%	UK Equity -29.9%	Japan Equity -0.2%

Global Govt Bonds 2.7%	Cash 5%	Global Govt Bonds -6.8%	Private Equity -6.7%	EM Equity - 36.6%	Timber - 0.2%
Timber 1.7%	Hedge Funds 4%	Japan Equity -7.7%	Japan Equity -9.5%	UK Property Shares - 46.6%	Gilts -1.2%
Gold -4.1%	Global Govt Bonds 3.8%	Commodities -14.6%	UK Property Shares - 36.7%	Private Equity - 64.3%	Global Govt Bonds -0.7%

Whilst a particular asset class may not be at the top of the table, it could still be a consistent performer. However, the Table shows that one cannot second-guess the investment market. It is a fact that the majority of investors do take past performance of an investment into account when making investment decisions – however, this can be risky as past performance is no guarantee of what may occur in the future.

Asset Allocation is therefore the main determinant of the investment mix.

Studies have shown that the biggest decision an investor makes is the allocation of funds to various asset classes, not the choice of individual securities (*Ibbotson & Associates*).

Volatility and investment returns

One must also take into account the volatility of investment returns. There is a view that all an investor need do is buy a collective investment portfolio and hold it for 20 years, accepting wide swings in investment performance. However, different asset classes perform differently at various phases of the economic cycle, for example gilts may outperform equities at different times. And also, some investments may fluctuate more widely than others. As a result, a standard deviation of a specific asset class is taken to measure its volatility and this is then compared to other asset classes. Standard deviation is an estimate of the likely divergence of an actual return from an expected return.

Market timing and rebalancing

Coupled with the above when making investments is that of market timing and the tactical rearrangement of asset classes, for example when you might miss a massive upturn in the market when sitting on cash. However, this is usually too difficult to call, and is replaced with the systematic rebalancing of asset classes to enhance performance, on a risk-adjusted basis. Portfolio construction decides on which asset classes to invest into and how much to invest into each asset class. Coupled with this is the choice of portfolio manager, or fund manager and the strategic weighting to be attached to each asset class. There are many books that have been written on making investments and how to get the best results and how to avoid risk-related catastrophes, and fund managers develop specialisms in their own areas of expertise. The fact is that very few fund managers are good all of the time, and many in fact fail to beat the market average on a consistent basis. Some of the principles mentioned above will give the reader a good insight into the basics of financial planning.

Risk

The concept of risk means different things to different people. There is financial planning risk (the risk of undertaking incorrect or no planning strategies); the risk of loss of capital; the risk that income will not keep pace with inflation; the risk of taxation decimating savings' income; the risk of investing into different markets or countries; and a host of other factors that influence or dictate risk. One of the major complaints to the FSA – the Financial Services Authority) is that investors did not understand the risks associated with an investment, and were therefore invested into the wrong investment.

Some many years ago, I did an in-depth study of risk and behaviour in relation to investors and their financial advisers. For the sake of simplicity, our standard of risk measurement was based on a scale of 1-10, where '1' is least risk – investing under the mattress, and '10' is most risky, investing into highly speculative investments. A '5' on this scale would be a balanced or medium risk taker. Investments associated with a medium risk taker would include at that time, endowment policies, some fixed interest investments, equities and property. In the discussion with the prospective client, I was assured by the client that he was a medium risk taker. This was my concept of what he should be after our discussion. However, it later transpired that his concept of a '5' or balanced investor was 50% invested in the Post Office and 50% in the building society. We cannot therefore make any assumptions in respect of a client's risk profile. This will also vary depending on his or her circumstances. Today an investor may be an aggressive investor as he has a lump sum to invest at age 35 for 25 years; however, tomorrow he may be aged 60 and about to retire, and cannot afford any risk to his capital.

A whole industry has been spawned by software companies who have developed risk analysis and risk- rating programmes for individuals. The problem is that unless the products or investments themselves have been risk-rated, one could still have a miss-match.

The following factors need to be considered when determining an investor's risk profile. Note that risk will never be eliminated, but it can be diversified so that the impact of making a wrong investment decision or strategy can be reduced.

- Understand *the relationship* between risk and return. This is fundamental. Low returns are usually associated with low risk and high returns command a higher risk profile.

- The *term* of the investment. The longer the term, the longer the risk may be absorbed. You may not be able to recoup losses if the investment is too short term.

- The *health* of the investor is important. Will cash be required for medical expenses? Will the investor be able to invest for short term periods only?

- Level of available *income* (and benefits). Those with high income and increasing income could sustain higher risk funds, as they have an income cushion. Those on benefits may lose benefits if the investment produces too much income or capital, if means-tested.

- The *age* of the investor is important. The younger the investor, the higher the level of risk that can be absorbed to absorb any returns. However, the reason for the investment is also important – if saving to buy a car you may only wish to be in a safe investment for say 2-3 years. Note also that today's 65 year old could live for at least another 20-30 years, and would also need growth investments – even though older ages are usually associated with lower risk profiles, this is not always the case. Age may also be a barrier. For example, if under age 16 you cannot have a cash ISA, or over age 89/90 you may not qualify for a discounted gift trust investment.

- *Other investments* being held are important. Are there sufficient reserves for an emergency? I have clients whose risk profile is usually cautious. However, for certain investments they insist on a higher level of risk for some of their money. So we also have the choice of whether to stick rigidly to your risk profile or not. Perhaps the client has already exceeded his investment allowance for a particular type of investment, such as an ISA, and cannot do anything more this tax year.

Risk profiling categories

Different risk profiling systems use different categories to classify investment risk. These range from:

1. *Conservative*
2. *Prudent*
3. *Moderate*
4. *Venturesome*
5. *Aggressive*

to

1. *Ultra Conservative – very low capital risk*
2. *Very Conservative – very low capital risk*

3. *Conservative – very low capital risk*
4. *Cautious – low risk*
5. *Cautious to Moderate – moderate risk*
6. *Moderate – medium risk*
7. *Moderate to Aggressive –medium to high risk*
8. *Aggressive – high risk*
9. *Speculative – very high risk*
10. *Very Speculative – exceptionally high risk*

Whilst risk can be measured mathematically, investors are also influenced by emotion. A financial planner usually finds that a client's tolerance for risk is lower than the client thinks it is. Most investors are actually loss averse rather than risk averse, and will accept poor returns as opposed to making capital losses.

An investment must be fit for purpose, and is usually purchased as part of general financial and investment planning. Investments can be risk rated, similarly with individuals, who themselves should be risk-rated.

Suggested asset allocation – balanced portfolio – long-term – 10 years +

- Higher risk earlier, reducing as fund usage time approaches
- UK shares – 60% (or 40% UK shares, 20% Property)
- International shares – 25%
- Bonds and gilts – 10%
- Cash, fixed interest – 5%

Suggested asset allocation – balanced portfolio – medium-term – 5 to 10 years

- Low to medium risk funds
- UK shares – 55% (or 40% UK shares, 15% property)
- International shares – 20%
- Bonds and gilts – 20%
- Cash, fixed interest – 5%

Suggested asset allocation – balanced portfolio – short-term – below 5 years

- Bonds and gilts – 75% (or 60% bonds and gilts, 15% property)
- Cash, fixed interest – 25%

These asset allocation examples may be typical of a cautious to moderate and moderate investor, seeking a balanced portfolio.

Investment advice process

Generally in financial planning, the investment advice process sits at the end of the financial planning process, using available cash resources. I use a simple '4 Pillar Philosophy' to determine *order of priority* for available cash:

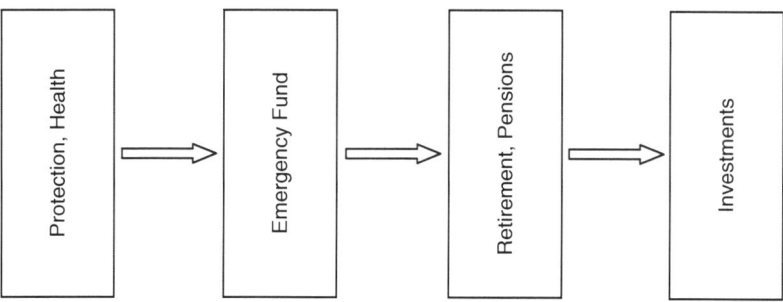

If advising a young married couple with minor children, you would start with family protection for available cash, moving through the main categories.

If an elderly person, who is single, without dependants, already retired, you would consider emergency funds first, then investments.

I often get new clients who call to say they wish to make an ISA investment, for example, of £10,200. As a financial planner, I must go through the process of confirmation and justification with the client first. If I find it's a young married couple with minor children, who have no life assurance for family protection and a mortgage with no protection, I will first consider their protection and health needs, then an emergency fund (which could be filled by the ISA), then retirement planning, and finally investments using their available cash. Whilst this couple wished to invest into ISA's when their need requirements are uncovered, there are far more serious considerations to make. Of course, it is the client's choice to say he is aware of these needs, but still wants that ISA investment to be made. So long as the financial planner and the client agree, the investment can be regardless – but at least the correct process has been followed. Your bank or stockbroker is unlikely to go through the process of needs analysis and requirements with you – they will merely sell you the product asked for.

The role of investments in financial planning

Investments are considered and made for different reasons. The main ones are:

- To provide growth for the investor
- To provide income for the investor
- To satisfy objectives – provide for secure income in retirement, provide for school fees, pay for nursing home costs, are examples.

- To reduce taxes – certain investments reduce tax or defer tax.
- To benefit others – investments can be set up for others, such as children

However, any investment made should be:

- Fit for purpose
- Within investor risk profiles
- Within cost, yields and term profiles
- And part of a
- An asset allocation process, which is diversified.

The investment universe is huge. The investment universe is diverse. It is full of danger for the unwary, who could lose their capital.

All is not always what it seems.

That safe, innocuous ISA or SIPP, could lose its tax status, for example. Funds could go missing (viz Keydata). Guarantees are also not what they purport to be. Purportedly safe funds may be suspended in times of crisis and can lose value, as happened with the Arch Cru funds debacle in recent times. The role of investment advisers is not to trust anything, and to question everything – and to document that they have done so. Investors are certainly more aware now that some investments can go wrong, and they do.

Even bank and building society deposits could be at risk, if a bank or building society fails. As a last resort there are investor protections – currently £50,000 of a bank deposit is protected and this will soon rise to E100,000 per person.

Proper investment planning is therefore essential, taking the circumstances, need requirements and objectives of the investor into account.

Investor compensation schemes

Investors are protected as follows for authorised investments in the UK (offshore jurisdictions either have investor compensation or they do not):

Banks and deposit-takers

Protection for depositors will increase in January 2011.

The current limit for Deposits is £50,000. The FSCS limit for deposits will increase on 31 December 2010 following European legislation. The FSA plan to issue a consultation shortly on increasing the coverage limit to the equivalent of 100,000. (Euros)- around £79,000.

Banks and building societies

Those which are licensed by the *Financial Services Authority* since 7 October 2008 are covered by a compensation scheme for 100% of up to

£50,000 per person for all accounts in each bank or building society. So for a joint account with two investors the limit is £100,000. However so far all the banks which have got into trouble have had *all* deposits to private investors paid back – the excess over £50,000 being paid for by the Government.

UK authorised insurance companies

These have the best protection for life and pensions policies. *The Financial Services Compensation Scheme* gives 100% on the first £2,000 and 90% on the rest.

UK authorised unit trusts and OEICs, ISAs (other than Cash ISAs), Personal Equity Plans, Friendly societies.

The Financial Services Compensation Scheme covers each investor for 100% of losses up to £30,000 and for 90% of the next £20,000 making a maximum payment of £48,000. This applies to investments made no earlier than 18 December 1986. There is no compensation for a fall in unit or share prices, only if there is a loss due to mismanagement or fraud by the managers.

2

Tax Allowances and Rates

What follows is a synopsis of the areas that should be looked at for investors to make the most use of tax deductions, and allowances available to them. Tax rates are also shown for various income levels, so that investors can determine how much the Treasury makes from their investments. The key aspects of the 2010 Budgets are also outlined and any subsequent changes, or expected changes.

Sir Winston Churchill: "There is no such thing as a good tax."

John Maynard Keynes: "The avoidance of taxes is the only intellectual pursuit that carries any reward."

Mark Twain: "The only difference between a taxman and a taxidermist is that the taxidermist leaves the skin."

British households waste £9.3 billion a year by paying too much tax, according to a recent report by IFA Promotion (IFAP). With 25 million households in the UK, this amounts to a tidy £372 per household per year.

Key Budget changes

24th March Budget 2010

For 2010/11

- Annual Allowance for pension contributions rises to £255,000 per person per year and frozen to 2015/16. *This has now been cut back to £50,000 from 6.4.2011.*
- Lifetime allowance rises to £1.8 million and is frozen to 2015/16. *This has now been cut back to £1.5 million from 6.4.2011.*
- Personal allowance is withdrawn at £1 for every £2 of income above £100,000 earnings.
- Additional rate of tax of 50% on taxable income over £150,000, and an additional rate on dividend income of 42.5%.
- From 2010/11 the ISA savings limits were increased to £10,200 each per tax year (of which £5,100 can be in cash). The limits are to rise with the RPI from April 2011.
- Confirmation of previous budgets that from 2011/12 tax relief on pension contributions for individuals with income over £150,000 will be gradually tapered. At £180,000 you will only receive basic rate relief (20%) on contributions. Total income is before deduction for pension contributions and charitable donations. If your income is £130,000 and over and together with your employer pension contributions takes you to £150,000

or over, your pension tax reliefs will be tapered. Anti-forestalling measures came into effect for 2009/10 and 2010/11 to prevent pension contribution increases before the new rules came into effect. The special annual allowance of £20,000 – £30,000 (depending on your circumstances) should cease to apply *after* the 2010/11 tax year (as the tapered pension relief rates come in then). *[Note that it has recently been announced that the maximum contribution will be £50,000 from 6.4.2011 and that relief will not be tapered, so up to 50% tax relief is available.]*

- The inheritance tax nil rate band is frozen at £325,000 to 6.4.2015.

22nd June 2010 Budget

- Personal tax allowances frozen at 2009/10 rates for 2010/11.
- Increases in personal allowance for those under age 65 by £1,000 to £7,475 in 2011/12.
- Capital gains tax on gains after 22.6.2010, for individuals a new higher rate of 28% where total taxable income and gains are above £37,400 – the higher rate applies to gains exceeding the limit. The personal allowance and losses reduce the gain. Where total taxable income and gains do not exceed the limit, gains remain taxable at 18%. For trustees and personal representatives, all taxable gains are taxed at 28%.
- Entrepreneur's relief is increased to £5 million from 23.6.2010 (the previous budget increased this to £2 million), and gains above that are taxed at 10%.
- The Government confirms the restrictions to pension contribution relief in the Finance Act 2010 for 2011/12 onwards by high income individuals. The Government is considering reducing the pension annual allowance from £255,000 to a range of £30,000 to £40,000. *This has in fact now been confirmed at £50,000 maximum pension contributions in any one year that attracts tax reliefs. Tax relief will not be tapered for high earners who can deduct contributions at up to 50%.*
- From 2011/12 the need to buy an annuity by age 75 moves to age 77; income drawdown limits will also extend to age 77; IHT charges where a member dies on or after age 75 will also be affected. In other words, the USP band will move to age 77, and ASP will be from age 77 from 6.4.2012. These are interim measures whilst a consultation process commences.
- The National Employment Savings Trust (NEST) – which is the new name for the employee compulsory pensions savings scheme (formerly Personal Accounts) will allow tax relief for employee and employer contributions from the date of the next Finance Act.
- The Government is considering removing the default retirement age of 65, but this will not be before 2011.

- **State Pension**
  Claimant   £97.65 per week (£5077.80 p.a.)
  Adult dependant   £58.50 per week (£3042 p.a.)
  Total married   £156.15 per week (£8,119.80 p.a.)
- The basic state pension increases by 2.5% from April 2010. The Government confirmed a triple guarantee for the basic state pension. From April 2010 it will be increased by the higher of the increase in prices, earnings or 2.5%.
- **Pensions Credit** if married or civil partnership.
  Guarantee Credit:
  Single   £132.60   (£6,895.20 pa)
  Couple   £202.40   (£10,524.80)

Post Budget Key Announcement 15 July 2010

The Government announces it proposed to end the rules forcing pension investors to buy an annuity at a specific age. This will take effect from 6th April 2011. It proposes capped and flexible drawdown options before and after age 75, making it unnecessary to offer alternatively secured pensions (ASP). You may even be allowed tax-free cash in *excess* of 25% so long as a minimum income is secured to prevent pensioners running out of funds. Announcements were also made on taxation of funds on death pre and post age 75, and inheritance tax applying to funds.

From the 2009 Budget relevant to this tax year 2010/11

- There is an increase in the upper earnings limit for class 1 and class 4 national insurance contributions from £770 to £844 per week. This affects rebates to pension schemes and calculations for salary sacrifice for pension contribution purposes. [same for 2010/11]
- NI contribution tax rises from 11% to 11.5% for individuals from April 2011.
- Higher rate income tax relief on pension contributions will be abolished from 2011/12 tax year. If earning over £150,000, above that level tax relief tapers to £180,000 where basic rate tax relief applies. *[note that this has now been superceded by a new Treasury announcement that the additional rate tax relief will apply (without taper) at 50% so long as the pension contribution is below £50,000 – from 6.4.2011]*
- There are interim measures for the 2009/10 tax year through a Special Annual Charge of 20%. This applies if your income exceeds £150,000 in this tax year, *or in any of the two previous tax years*. Income for this purpose is total income for the tax year before pension contributions, personal allowances, or any other reliefs or deductions (gross income from all sources). You can deduct reliefs such as trading losses, including deductions for pension contributions up to a maximum of £20,000, less any gift aid deductions. You then add any income foregone by a salary sacrifice arrangement in return for pension

contributions entered into on or after 22nd April 2009. Contributions paid before 23rd April 2009 are excluded from the 2009/10 tax year.

- The Special Annual Allowance (SAA) is £20,000 per year. This includes employer's contributions and defined benefit scheme accrual (calculated in the same way as a Pension Input amount for Annual Allowance purposes). Any input in excess of the SAA will be subject to the SAA charge of 20%. Existing tax reliefs continue to be available to all whose input amount in a tax year is £20,000 or less.

- There are two exemptions: (i) where regular contributions currently exceed £20,000 p.a. – *no* SAA charge if regular premiums continue to be paid, and must be paid at least quarterly to qualify as regular contributions, and (ii) where the member retires on the grounds of ill health or dies before the end of the tax year.

- From 22nd April 2009 UK investors with distributions from offshore funds with more than 40% in equities will receive a non-payable dividend tax credit. (This reinstates the tax credit for offshore funds announced in the 2008 budget). Basic rate taxpayers will pay no further tax. Higher rate taxpayers will be liable to a further 25% income tax based on the net dividend received. If however, the offshore fund is invested in more than 60% in interest-bearing assets, no tax credit is available. In this case the distribution is treated as interest and taxed at 20% for basic rate taxpayers and 40% for higher rate taxpayers; 50% for additional rate taxpayers. Also, individuals receiving dividends from non-resident UK companies will be entitled to a non payable tax credit (from a qualifying territory).

- From 6th April 2010 non-UK resident individuals will *not* qualify for UK personal allowances or reliefs by reason of being Commonwealth citizens (but may still qualify for double taxation relief). This could make pensions payable to those living abroad more expensive as more tax could be payable.

- From 6th April 2009 EIS tax relief can be related back to the previous tax year at 100%. So if the maximum £500,000 was invested, income tax relief of £100,000 can be related back to the previous tax year. Investments need no longer be made by 6th October in the tax year. This may help high earners, who will be limited in their pension contributions in the future to seek additional tax reliefs.

Main tax allowances and exemptions (2010/11)

Personal Allowances – Income Tax

Under age 65 :   £6,475
Age 65 -74:   £9,490
Age 75 and over: £9,640

These allowances reduce taxable income. Note that from £100,000 the personal allowance is reduced on a £1-for-£1 basis on income over £100,000 from 6th April 2010, and from 6th April 2010 those earning £150,000 or more will pay income tax at 50%.

From 6th April 2010, the personal allowance which is restricted for individuals with a net adjusted income of £100,000+ tapers to nil, and the effective tax rate becomes 60% between £100,000 and £112,950. There is therefore a great need for tax planning to reduce taxable income sufficiently so that it is below £100,000, where possible.

Personal Allowances that reduce tax: Married couples allowance (MCA) if one claimant born before 6th April 1935, so only now if age 75 and over: £696.50

UK personal allowances and reliefs for non-UK residents have been removed from 6th April 2010. This will affect Commonwealth citizens, who previously were allowed these reliefs.

If age 75 and over there are age relief penalties that apply that reduce your personal allowance on a £1-for-£1 basis if you have taxable income over £22,900. However, the personal allowance cannot reduce to below the lowest personal allowance of £6,475.

Savings income

Note that the 10% starting rate is only available for savings income up to £2,440. It is not applicable if taxable non savings income exceeds £2,440.

Income tax rates (2010/11)

Category	On first £2,440	Next £34,960	Next £112,600	Above £150,000
Earnings, pensions, property	20%	20%	40%	50%
Savings	10%	20%	40%	50%
Dividends	10%	10%	32.5%	42.5%

Capital Gains Tax

Capital Gains Tax is payable on taxable gains above the personal allowance. There is no indexation or taper reliefs for individuals. Capital gains tax on gains after 22nd June 2010, for individuals a new higher rate of 28% where total taxable income and gains are above £37,400 – the higher rate applies to gains exceeding the limit. The personal allowance and losses reduce the gain. Where total taxable income and gains do not exceed the limit, gains remain taxable at 18%. For trustees and personal representatives, all taxable gains are taxed at 28%.

Annual exempt amount

Per person: £10,100
Trustees: £5,050
(divided up to 5 trusts)

Tax is a flat rate of 18% up to £37,400 (total taxable income and taxable gains), and at 28% above that level for individuals. Trusts and deceased estates (personal representatives) pay tax at the higher rate of 28%. The trust CGT allowance reduces for trusts established by the same Settlor by dividing the amount of the allowance by the number of trusts concerned.

Entrepreneurs' relief

Entrepreneur's relief is increased to £5 million from 23.6.2010 (the previous budget increased this to £2 million), and gains above that are taxed at 10%. This would apply to an entrepreneur satisfying the criteria for relief on selling a business, and is a concession recently increased by the Government.

Companies

The exempt amount or allowance for capital gains is not available to companies. Capital gains can be reduced through loss reliefs and indexation. The capital gain is added to the company's income and taxed at the corporation marginal rate of tax applying.

Capital gains investments

Even though the underlying investments may be subject to capital gains tax when realised or disposed of, there is an element of tax efficiency through using investments that produce capital gains, because of the use of the CGT personal allowance.

Individuals each have a CGT exemption of £10,100 in 2010/11.

Trusts have an exemption of half that rate of £5,050 (split between up to 5 trusts).

Many investments provide for capital gains as opposed to taxable income. A married couple could have £20,200 in this tax year as tax-free 'income' from capital gains. Non taxable income can therefore be produced from taking taxable gains within the personal and trust allowances you may have annually. Do not confuse a 'gain' with a tax – your investments may still be liable to income tax on savings income and dividends.

Capital gains tax may be deferred through investing the gain into a qualifying investment, such as an EIS investment. CGT is therefore an optional tax and may never be paid, as it dies with the individual – so long as you keep deferring it. Each year, you can crystallise so much of the gain to use up your personal allowance for that year, whilst continuing with the deferral process.

Pension contributions

From 2011/2012

From 6.4.2011 – if income is above £150,000 – tax relief on pension contributions is given at the additional rate of 50%, but only for a maximum amount of £50,000. Until then, taper relief applies between £150,000 and £180,000 where relief is at 20%, and the anti-forestalling rules are in force until 5.4.2011.

Rent-a-room relief

Income from renting out a room in your house is tax-free up to £4,250.

This must be your principal residence to qualify. It does not affect the sale of your house, which, as your principal private residence will be tax-free.

Approved employee share option schemes

The increase of the exercise price of the option over the value at the grant of the option will be tax-free subject to the rules.

Redundancy payments

Payments may be made tax-free up to £30,000. There is no tax and NI if a genuine redundancy payment.

Making use of your allowances

You may have taxable investments, however your personal allowances would render all or part of them tax-free.

Personal Allowances

Under age 65:	£6,475
65 -74:	£9,490
75 and over:	£9,640

Age related allowances are progressively withdrawn if taxable income exceeds £22,900.

Capital Gains Tax Allowance: £10,100 per person. Trusts have an exemption of £5,050.

Gains (growth) can be taken free of taxes at up to this amount. Check investments for capital gains and possibly dispose of enough to satisfy this allowance. Some growth investments can be used to provide annual income in this way.

Capital Gains are taxed at rates of 18% or 28%, depending on your income. However, if in the last 3 years you have paid CGT at 40%, then investing into an EIS to defer CGT will also return the tax paid at 40%. Once the event is crystallised, the investment can be sold (e.g. AIM Shares) and tax paid at 18% or 28%.

Register capital losses with HMRC to carry forward and offset against gains arising in future tax years.

Assign assets to a spouse or civil partner paying a lower rate of income tax, or with unused allowances, before realising life policy or capital gains.

Claim your tax credits

Up to £3.7 billion of tax credits are on offer from HM Revenue & Customs (HMRC) and the Department for Work and Pensions. To find out if you can claim Child Tax Credit, Working Family Tax Credit or Pension Credit, visit the independent **EntitledTo** website. Nine in ten families can claim some kind of help via tax credits. However, you will see this door begin to close in the future as the Government carries out its benefit reductions across the board.

Claim back savings tax

HMRC automatically grabs a fifth (20%) of your **savings** interest 'at source' – before you receive it. So, if you're a non-taxpayer or only pay tax at 10%, then you could be paying too much tax. Get a form R40 from the taxman and claim what's owed – you can go back as far as 2004/05. In addition, fill in a form R85 at your bank or building society to stop future overpayments. This would save three million people with low earnings a total of £330 million a year.

Be smart with your spouse

If you pay tax but have a non-taxpaying wife or husband or civil partner, then you can save tax by transferring income-generating assets into his/her name. Every adult has a tax-free allowance of at least £6,475 in the 2010/11 tax year, so make sure that your other half's allowance doesn't go to waste. £144 million could be saved by redistributing savings in this way. Another £264 million could be saved by making use of spouses' Capital Gains Tax allowance (£10,100 for 2010/11).

3

Tax and Investments

Inflation and tax can seriously affect your investment returns.

If the investment is taxable, that reduces the actual return. The real value is further reduced by inflation.

Inflation

CPI is at 3.1% (this is the consumer price index); and RPI is at 4.6% (retail prices index) in September 2010. CPI replaced RPI as the official inflation figure in 2003. RPI includes mortgage interest payments. The highest RPI inflation recorded in the last 40 years was in 1975 at 26.9% in August 1975, and the lowest was in June 2009 at -1.6%. Inflation is therefore one of the greatest risks against your savings.

The objective of the investor should be to beat inflation in real terms. However, if the investment was not taxed, then the investor has a greater chance of beating inflation.

An interesting statistic is that inflation is also higher or lower depending on your social and economic status. For example, the cost of certain goods and services purchased by different age and economic groups can vary widely, depending on what they purchase. Older people may need more heat in winter and increasing fuel prices could mean they have less to spend in other areas. The level of state pension has been pegged at the RPI level of inflation in the past, but now reverts to the CPI, a lower level. So expect less in real terms. Similarly, a worker with travel costs that increase on a regular basis, such as petrol, diesel and rail fares, will find the value of his money worth less.

Is inflation an intrinsically bad thing? Economists and treasury officials seem to think it is. However, if you are in the housing market and want the best price for your house, you will think house inflation is a good thing – unless you use the proceeds of your house sale to buy another house in an inflated economy. Keeping inflation down is a prime concern of fiscal policy and the Government target is 2%, and it uses interest rates to control inflation. The bank base rate has been at 0.5% for some time now, and is expected to rise by at least 0.5% to 0.75% over the next 18 months.

Financial planners tend to assume around 3% for inflation as an average to be expected going forward in these times, when calculating the effect of inflation on your savings and investments.

With the rise in interest rates expected, this could be better news for savers. However, to beat inflation, one needs to be in investments that grow, not stand still. If invested in banks and building societies, you will not be too shocked to know that savers are losing out on some £12 billion in interest when holding money in savings accounts or current accounts. Which? Says 50% of the 1,200 plus savings accounts in the UK today paid interest of 0.5% or less, whilst 25% pay just 0.1% or lower. If all savers moved to the highest paying accounts, consumers would collectively receive an extra £12 billion per year of £22 each (*Shropshire Star 21.10.10*)

Savers seeking to index-link their investments to safeguard them against inflation, rushed to invest into index-linked bonds with National Savings and Investments (NS&I), and in July 2010, overwhelmed by savers, the investment was closed to new investors. The NS&I (backed by HM Treasury and 100% secure) saw a near-record £5.4bn inflow of money in the first quarter of this year. The bonds are held by 580,000 customers with £17bn deposited, and typically pay a rate of inflation as measured by the Retail Prices Index (RPI) plus 1%. Existing customers were not be affected by the move.

With RPI at about 5% then, and the bonds offering tax-free interest, the three- and five-year certificates had seen a surge in demand. NS&I also cut interest rates with immediate effect on its direct saver and income bonds by 0.25%, reducing rates to between 1.45% and 1.75%.

With little choice available for safe and secure index-linking investments, and now further restricted, the investor may look to alternatives, such as structured products – but these do not have the same security as the NS & I offered index-linked bonds.

What then is the effect of inflation on your money?

Assume inflation is at 3.1% (the current CPI figure). You have a bank account earning 3.5%. The real return before tax on your money is 0.4%. If a 20% taxpayer, then 20% x 3.5% is 2.8%. Take off inflation at 3.1% and your return is in negative territory in real terms.

One also needs to consider capital gains tax. Whilst the first £10,100 of your capital gain is tax-free, the balance could be taxable at between 18% and 28% depending on your tax status. Assume you are a 28% capital gains tax payer and you have already used your annual allowance, and inflation is at 3.1%, then:

You invested £100,000 and the investment grew by 10%. You decide to take the gain, which is £10,000. After tax of 28%, you are left with £7,200. After applying inflation, this is now worth £6,976.

Tax on investments

Since the maximum rate of income tax is 50% and the maximum rate of capital gains tax is 28% (compared to the minimum savings rate of tax of 10% and capital gains tax of 18%); and the rate of dividend taxation ranges from 10% to 42.5%, it may make sense to invest for capital gains, rather than for taxable interest or dividends, especially if a higher or additional rate taxpayer. In other words, a return based on capital growth may be more attractive than a return based on income or dividends.

Everyone's circumstances are different, and therefore their investment strategies will differ.

Many investors fear the risk of investing in shares or collective investments with equities (recent stock market falls and losses experienced will still be in their memory banks) because they firmly believe they will lose their money and resort to fixed interest type investments. They may be unaware of the effect of tax and inflation on their investments, but are comforted by the security of their capital and nominal rates of interest received.

It is sound advice to not base your investment decisions solely on tax considerations. In fact many 'investments' are tax mitigation schemes and not really investments. Some may succeed, and others may go spectacularly wrong. The debacle at Canary Wharf when investors bought into an enterprise zone trust investment many years ago, which was highly geared (the bank lent them money to invest with the rental income supposed to service the bank interest and loan), and when tenants deserted the properties, no income was received and the banks foreclosed, with losses to investors.

The previous chapter outlined the various tax rates applying to income and dividends, and also capital gains tax applying for individuals and trusts.

However, some entities do not pay any tax at all on the investment income from interest or dividends, or even on capital gains. Qualifying pension funds grow completely tax-free, so do venture capital trusts, and so do ISA investments. Housing your investment in the correct vehicle or tax wrapper could improve investment returns considerably.

One must consider the tax status of the various receiving entities of investments. These would be individuals, trusts and companies.

The status of the investment is also important. An investment fund with distributor status, for example, could be subject to capital gains tax, whereas one without distributor status, would be subject to income tax.

Individuals

Investments may be categorised through tax allowances or the product itself having a certain tax status. For example, an investment may be taxable, but still be tax-efficient because of a capital gains tax exemption, or an income tax personal allowance which the individual may have. When advising a person, the financial planner must take into account all the circumstances of the individual, complete an investment risk analysis, determine the tax status and available allowances. Age is important as the personal allowance is reduced for the over-65-year-old with income of over £22,900. Tax therefore does play a major part in investment selection. Non taxpayers may have tax-free returns from taxable investments, because of their personal allowances. Investments may be taxed at rates from 10% to 50% for income, 10% to 42.5% for dividends and 18% to 28% for capital gains.

Trusts

Trusts have been particularly hard hit by recent tax changes. Trust tax rates have increased to 50% on all income (bar the first £1,000), and 42.5% on all dividends. Unlike an individual investor who gets to the 50% tax rate at £150,000, trusts suffer penal tax at this rate after £1,000. Dividends are taxed at 42.5%. Even if you do not take the income from an investment, and it is reinvested, the trust is taxed on that income. In certain instances, the beneficiary of the trust can claim back tax paid by the trustees, if his or her tax rate is lower. This could reduce the incidence of trust taxation. Capital gains are taxed at 28% in a trust. Trustees generally cannot hold cash for too long – they must have an investment policy. The problem for many trusts – especially discretionary trusts- is that the tax take will eat up half the income and almost the same with dividends. The alternative will be to take capital gains at 28% or defer taxation through an investment bond. The section on trusts covers different scenarios for different types of trusts. Trusts have a capital gains tax exemption of half of the individual exemption, currently £5,050 split between the number of trusts to a maximum of five trusts with the same Settlor. Trusts can invest into an EIS to defer capital gains tax, but are precluded from the income tax relief that an individual may receive.

Companies

Companies can make investments, and indeed they do. Any income received is added to other corporation income and taxed at that rate. Similarly for capital gains.

Companies are taxed on profits as follows (to 31st March 2011):

0-£300,000 at 21%
£300,001 to £1,500,000 at 29.75%
£1,500,001 and over at 28%

Investments such as corporate venturing are tax deductible to a company.

Companies may invest in a number of diverse areas and have 100% tax allowances, or have the investment tax relievable against profits. An individual can have the use of company assets, and would, in most cases pay benefit in kind taxation (however this usually only applies if you earn more than £8,500 per annum).

Having an understanding of the tax position of the entity receiving income, dividends or gains, or providing the use of an asset is important when it comes to investment decision- making.

4

Tax-Efficient Investments for Individuals

In dealing with tax-efficient investments for individuals, there are a number of different categories to consider. Investments can be tax-free in whole or part, or tax-reducing, thus increasing returns, and even taxable, but your personal allowances or deductions could make it equally as efficient as a tax-free investment. Other investments may be tax-deferred, often for long periods, or until death. Each of these categories has a role to play in the investment planning process for tax efficiency. Ultimate tax efficiency is to use the tax system for best advantage for the investor, depending on his or her circumstances.

Tax-Free Investments

Tax-Reducing Investments

Taxable, but Efficient Investments

Tax-Deferred Investments

5

Tax-Free Investments

These are investments that grow tax-free, or mature tax-free, or have tax-free income, or even non taxable gains.

The following investments are covered in this section:

- ISA's – Individual Savings Accounts
- Certain National Savings products
- Friendly Society Investment Policies
- MIPs and endowment policies
- Child's Trust Fund and the new Junior ISA
- Forestry Investments
- Pensions
- Your Family Home
- Spread bets/FX trades
- Annuities
- SAYE
- Zeros

ISA investments

An ISA – Individual Savings Account – is an investment that offers two main choices. You can either invest into a cash account (for half of the ISA allowance only), or into stocks and shares (investment ISA) for the full amount or the other half of the cash account to make up the total investment of £10,200 per person for this tax year. The investment grows completely tax-free and income may be taken from it tax-free. It can be sold at any time and there is no maximum or minimum term. You can have a cash ISA from age 16 and an investment ISA from age 18. It has recently been announced that a Junior ISA will be available for youngsters to take the place of the CTF (Child Trust Fund), but will not be funded by the Government. No details are available at this stage.

Investments can be made by lump sum, or some investment providers allow regular savings into ISA accounts. Since April 1999, more than 18 million people have invested over £180 billion into ISAs to take advantage of the tax perks. There is no capital gains tax payable on investment growth or withdrawal, which can be at any time, and income can be taken tax-free.

There are two investment components – cash, and stocks and shares. You can invest the whole £10,200 annual allowance into stocks and shares each year; or £5,100 into cash, and £5,100 into stocks and shares. You must be aged 18 or over to have an ISA (except for the age 16 for a cash ISA).

Cash ISAs can be invested on fixed or variable rates.

In 2006, Ed Balls announced ISAs are to stay indefinitely.

The ISA is the UK's most popular tax shelter. From 6.4.2010 the amount of ISA investment rises by £960 for the 2011/12 tax year to £11,160 per person. A couple could therefore invest up to £20,400 free from tax in the 2010/11 tax year and in the following tax year £22,320. The government has confirmed that it would index link the annual ISA subscription limit from 2011/12.

Once you die, that's the end of your ISA as well. Any savings or investments you had in them become taxable from the date of your death and they are included in your estate for inheritance tax purposes.

ISAs can be transferred from one provider to another, without losing tax reliefs. At the time of writing, the following are the best ISA rates for cash ISAs:

- **Santander** – instant access at 2.85%, interest paid annually and minimum is £1
- **Halifax and Principality** – no notice at 2.80%, interest paid annually and minimum is £1
- **Bank of Cyprus UK** – fixed rate 1 year at 3%, interest paid on maturity and minimum £1
- **Northern Rock** – fixed rate 1 year at 2.85%, interest paid annually, minimum £500
- **Bank of Cyprus** – fixed rate 3 years at 4.15%, interest at end minimum £1
- **Halifax** – fixed rate 4 years at 4.25%, interest at end, minimum £500

Beware – some institutions offer a low annual rate but have a bonus at the end, if you stay the course.

National Savings Investments

NS & I are guaranteed by the Government, and are therefore very popular with savers, even though generally their rates do not match those of other savings institutions. Most of their tax-free investment products have been withdrawn due to unprecedented demand and the failure by the Treasury to guarantee any further investments for the time being, because of the spending cuts. However, as many investors will have these investments, they are shown below – especially as they may have the facility to roll over into new issues in the future, with similar tax-free guarantees.

Fixed interest savings certificates – 2 year 47th issue, guaranteed compound rate over 2 years paying 1.25% AER, and tax-free – no issues available.

Fixed interest savings certificates, 5 year 96th issue, guaranteed compound rate over 5 years paying 2.25% AER, and tax-free – no issues available.

General Extension rate earned on 7th to 43rd issue Fixed interest savings certificates, that matured before 8 October 2001 and on Yearly Plan, for each complete period of 3 months, paying 0.09% AER, and tax-free – no issues available.

Index-Linked Savings Certificates , 5 year 46th issue, guaranteed compound rate over 5 years paying index-linking + 1% AER, and tax-free – (returns guaranteed to beat inflation, as measured by the RPI, when held for at least 1 year) – no issues available.

Children's Bonus Bonds Issue 34, guaranteed compound rate over 5 years including 5th anniversary bonus, and tax-free, paying 2.5% AER – *this is available*

You can invest tax-free for your child's future in their own name. All returns on Children's Bonus Bonds are completely tax-free for both child and parent. "Tax-free" means you don't have to pay any UK Income Tax or Capital Gains Tax. This can be cashed in early, but no interest is earned if cash in within the first year. The minimum deposit is £25, and the maximum in the account is £3,000, interest is paid on maturity and the rate is now 2.5%.

For regular investments, the Index-linked savings certificate 19th issue is a 3-year term, with a minimum investment of £100, which pays a fixed 1% p.a. + inflation (about 2.2%) tax-free; they therefore beat inflation, but not by much. This is currently not available.

Premium Bonds pay out a tax-free return.

Friendly Society policies

A Friendly Society policy is similar to an endowment policy, and in fact most use with profits funds. Restricted in the amount you can invest, the returns are tax-free if the investment runs for at least 10 years. The minimum investments are as low as £10 per month or £100 per annum, the maximum £25 per month or £250 per annum. Each child and parent per family can take out an investment of this type. Most invest into with-profits funds, however, Friendly Societies have special tax treatment and often their returns are better than conventional life offices. There is no minimum age, but the maximum is age 80. The investment fund is exempt from CGT, corporation and income taxes.

There are over 70 friendly societies to choose from, including those aimed at teachers, dentists, policemen, foresters, shepherds, Anglo-Saxons, children, and the like: see www.friendlysocieties,co.uk

MIPs and endowments

Maximum investment plans (MIPs)

Largely out of favour at present, but there are a few companies around with above-average returns. The monthly investment is into a life assurance policy for a minimum period of 10 years (although the proceeds can be withdrawn after seven and a half years, tax-free).

The returns are tax-free, but the life office will have suffered tax on its internal funds. All include life cover, with a payout on death. MIPs are unit-linked life assurance policies, with a large percentage of the premiums invested. The minimum age is age 12 and the maximum age is 80. You can take a tax-free income after ten years, so long as you continue to pay at least 50% of the original premium.

The minimum premium is from £20 per month, depending on the provider. If death occurs within the ten-year policy term, the greater of the guaranteed death benefit or the unitised investment fund will be paid.

The MIP provides a tax-free capital sum and tax-free income after ten years; the capital can be left to grow after ten years; and you can continue to pay premiums for a further ten years. Policies can be underwritten on a joint life basis, payable on first or second death. A series of MIPs can be taken out to mature at different dates when they will be required. Some may have loan facilities, should cash be needed earlier.

New entrants to the market place include Skandia. They compare investing in a MIP to investing in an OEIC and a pension scheme as follows:

	MIP	OEIC/Unit Trust	Pension
Contributions	No tax relief	No tax relief	Tax relief
Tax on income in wrapper	0-20% – varies depending on income	At individual's highest level 0-50% -income and dividends	Nil
Tax on growth in wrapper	0-20% – varies on type of gain	Nil – the 10% tax at source on UK dividends cannot be reclaimed	Nil
Tax on encashment	So long as hold for 10 years and premiums are maintained – no income or CGT on withdrawals or encashment	Gains over annual allowance taxed at 18% to 28%. If part withdrawals take place, use the part withdrawals formula to calculate gain.	25% of fund tax-free Balance in annuity/USP/ASP tax at marginal rate. Surcharges if income above lifetime allowance at 25% and 55% if taken as cash.

The MIP could be useful for high income earners (e.g. 50% taxpayers in 2010/11) and where there are tax restrictions on pension contributions and relief, and ISA allowances have been maximised.

Legal & General have recently launched their Portfolio Regular Investment Plan (PRIP), which consists of 100 policies, each one being certified as a 'qualifying policy' by HM Revenue & Customs. L&G said the policies are also "tax-favoured" and comply with HMRC rules on policy term, regularity and level of premiums, and a minimum amount payable on death, so it will not normally give rise to chargeable event gains.

After ten years, investors will be able to choose to cash in the plan in part or in full, hold it for further potential investment gain or continue to pay regular premiums for a further ten years. L&G said this flexibility means the PRIP is suitable for inheritance tax mitigation, repatriation of offshore investment and flexible tax-favoured solutions for saving for school or university fees.

The PRIP has a minimum investment of £1,000 a month or £12,000 a year. It also has an unbundled charging structure which allows advisers to agree a level of remuneration with clients best suitable to their business model.

Products such as the above are entering the market space for MIPs, with lower charging structures and more product features.

Endowment assurance policies

For those wishing to build up a tax-free lump sum over a long term, these policies offer a relatively low-risk investment medium to do so. The policy is for a minimum period of ten years for tax-free proceeds (although after seven and a half years proceeds can be withdrawn tax-free on a ten-year plan). Policies are either with profits or unit-linked, and a wide range of investment funds are usually offered.

Unlike Friendly Society policies, corporation tax and CGT will be charged on the income or capital gains arising on the life company's funds. You may also have to be medically examined, and life cover may be expensive. The charging structure could also be high, although providers are reducing charges to make their products more saleable. You must be aged between 12 to 75 years to effect an endowment assurance policy.

One must distinguish between endowments that are pure savings oriented with a minimum of life cover, as opposed to, say, one required for a mortgage, where the life cover requirement is higher. Early surrender could result in penalties and loss of investment capital, so view this as a longer-term investment.

You can also purchase a second-hand with-profits endowment policy and pay the premiums on it until maturity. The payout is free of income tax, but may be subject to capital gains tax, although you have an exemption of £10,100 per person in 2010/11.

Endowment policies have largely fallen out of favour over recent years, as a result of over-estimating returns, and have been seen as poor value.

However, Friendly Society policies are popular and MIPs may see a resurgence.

Child's Trust Funds

From April 2005, all children born after September 1st 2002 will have received a voucher from the Government to the value of £250 (from January 2005). If parents earn less than £15,575 a year, then the amount is £500. A further payment is made when the child reaches age 7. This money is to be invested into a Child's Trust Fund, which will have tax-free returns. Parents and grandparents, friends and family can add another £1,200 a year. The fund can be encashed from age 18. There is a wide range of investment options to choose from. These include stakeholder style products as well as cash-based schemes. For maximum growth potential, one would want exposure to equities.

Assuming an investment return of 6%, if the £250 was invested, with a further £1,200 a year to age 18, the value of the fund would be £39,577, enough to pay for 3 years at University.

Because the Government does not have the budget for CTFs, they are to be scrapped from 1.1.2010. Existing CTFs will be allowed to continue until maturity. It was recently announced that a Junior ISA will become available for young savers, but will not be funded by the Government.

Forestry investments/woodlands

Investing into forestry and woodlands is mainly for extremely passive investors with time on their hands. For most there will be returns after say 10 years. Direct investments in forestry are eligible for Business Property Relief (BPR), providing relief against IHT after two years.

There is no tax on harvested timber. There is no capital gains tax in the growth in value of the timber crop.

There is no income tax relief on newly purchased woodlands. There is no loss relief available. (Income is non-taxable). SDLT is payable on the purchase of woodland.

There are grants incentives available to all woodlands' investors.

The investment is seen as a low risk, asset backed investment. Returns are generated from harvesting the timber and the increase in land values. In 2008 the total return on investments in forestry was 7% (20% in 2006) – this outperformed equities and commercial property.

Investments are direct (where you get the tax benefits), or through unit trusts, Investment trusts, ETF's (exchange-traded funds) (where you do not get the tax benefits).

Collective funds include: Cambium Global Timberland, Phaunos Timber, Stellar Forestry Fund.

Pensions

Pensions are highly tax-efficient investment vehicles. Contributions are tax relievable for some, and the HMRC uplifts personal pension contributions by 20%, when made. The pension fund itself grows tax-free, and on maturity or retirement from the pension fund, 25% of the fund can be taken as a pension commencement lump sum (tax-free cash), payable tax-free. The balance of the fund purchases a pension that is taxable as income.

Anyone (even babies!) can make a pension contribution – even if you have no taxable income, a minimum contribution is allowed.

Whilst a minor can invest into a stakeholder pension, he or she will have to reach age 55 before being able to receive the fruits of such investment. Minors can invest (or their parents and grandparents for them), £3,600 each year into a stakeholder pension without the need for earnings. The investment is made net of 20% basic rate tax and the actual investment made is £2,880, with the HMRC adding the balance (£720) to make the contribution up to £3,600.

If the minor is a taxpayer, then the pension contribution reduces tax payable by increasing the basic rate tax band. Parents and grandparents can also make stakeholder pension contributions for the minor.

For those under age 55 at 2011

If you do not have a pension fund, make tax-deductible pension contributions to a retirement fund. Tax relief is given at your marginal rate of tax (HMRC could fund up to 50% of your pension fund in this way, if a higher rate taxpayer (40%) and 50% if an additional rate taxpayer. 20% is paid into your pension plan and 20%- 30% returned to you as tax savings). A basic rate or non-taxpayer has 20% added by HMRC to his pension contribution. Non-earning investors with only investment income only can invest up to £3,600 gross (£2,880 net) per annum under the stakeholder pension rules.

If over age 55

You can make annual single premium deductible pension contributions into a personal pension plan. Each year, you can take out the tax-free cash element (25% of the fund) and use this for any purpose, such as paying for school fees funding or for income. The balance of your fund is available to purchase a pension, most of which can be deferred until actual retirement date. The total tax relief for a higher rated taxpayer is 20% on the contribution plus an HMRC contribution of 20% – 30% to the pension fund, depending on your tax status. In addition, 25% in tax-free cash is available for each single premium pension payment made each year.

Both of the above methods give tax relief on your investment made, and could enable big earners to get their school and university fees for free, as well as going some way to meeting retirement objectives.

Taking tax-free cash from a pension fund for a guaranteed return of over 25%

This could be a useful investment strategy, if age over 55. Make a series of single premium contributions to a pension fund. The HMRC adds 20% to the investment. Immediately take the tax-free cash and defer the balance of the pension fund. The older you are the greater annual return if taking an annuity. If a 40% taxpayer, you get an additional 20% tax relief (if a 50% taxpayer, you get 30%) on your contribution, thus reducing the net cost of the investment even further.

Anyone up to the age of 75 *[the maximum age for tax relief is age 74]*(including children) can contribute to a pension and earn basic-rate tax relief of 20% or higher-rate tax relief of up to 50% on these contributions (depending on your income tax band). The upper limit for tax relief is currently 100% of your salary, up to a maximum contribution of £255,000 in the 2010/11 tax year. This relief is restricted by the anti-forestalling provisions to £20,000 to £30,000 in contributions depending on whether making regular payments or not, in 2010/11, if earning over £130,000. From 2011/12, the maximum contribution allowable will be £50,000, and the highest earners can claim tax relief at their marginal rates – up to 50%.

If your income is so low you don't have to pay tax, then your maximum pension contribution is capped at £3,600 per tax year. But you only actually need to contribute £2,880 to achieve a pension pot this size. This is because you still benefit from 20% basic-rate tax relief – provided b y the HMRC at £720.

Furthermore, if you are aged between 55 and 75 (you must currently take the tax-free cash by age 75, but the annuity age has shifted to age 77 from 2011/12, if ongoing drawdown has not been selected) then you can immediately withdraw a quarter (25%) of this pot as tax-free cash. In other words, you can get back £900 of your £3,600 straight away. So, after deducting the £720 tax relief and tax-free cash of £900, a net pension contribution of £1,980 provides you with a pension pot of £2,700.

You can then use this £2,700 pot to buy a pension annuity -- a guaranteed income paid by an insurance company until you die. You can choose to have this annuity income paid yearly in advance, which means that you can receive your first year's payment straight away. Note that annuity rates increase with age and women are paid lower rates than men, simply because females live longer.

So, by making full use of pension tax relief, tax-free cash and yearly annuities, you can earn super-high -- yet secure -- returns on your spare cash. Here's a table of possible returns on offer based on £2,700 invested into a single annuity for income for life (non smoker- *If a smoker, rates will increase):*

Current age (male)	Yearly income (£)	Yearly return (%)	Current age (female)	Yearly income (£)	Yearly return (%)
60	149.85	5.55	60	143.91	5.33
65	167.94	6.22	65	157.68	5.84
70	195.75	7.25	70	182.25	6.75
75	233.55	8.65	75	214.11	7.93

Source: Aviva. These annuity quotes are from Aviva at 29th October 2010 at £10,000 based on £2,700, non smoker single life only; annuity rates from other insurers may differ. These rates are illustrative only.

As you can see, a 75-year-old male can get a (taxable) income of £233.55 a year for life by buying an annuity with £2,700, an annual return on the annuity amount invested of 8.65% taxable. The total first-year return is 25% (tax-free cash) + 8.65% income = 33.65% on a net cost after tax-free cash is returned of £1,980. Thereafter the return is 8.65% for life in this example. The income return alone, based on the net cost of £1,980 is 11.79% [233.55/1,980].

The best low risk tax investment – ever

(Source: A recent article by Tony Granger, published by Tax Insider October 2010)

'A pension can often be the longest running financial commitment that most of us will have. But with the recent bad press and the complex, ever changing rules, are they still worth investing into?

With profound volatility on investment funds still remembered following the recent stock market crash and credit crunch crisis, many remain wary about where to invest their funds.

Get a 20% return immediately from HMRC

Pensions are an interesting investment. It is one of the very few investments where the Government adds 20% to what you invest, whether a taxpayer or not. So for the pension contribution you make, the State adds 20%. That's a 20% return on your investment before it even starts earning you money! Better still, if a higher rate taxpayer (with taxable income of over £37,400 in 2010/11), then a further 20% of your investment comes back to you through the tax system [*and 30% if earning over £150,000*].

So pensions can be great investments. If aged 55 and above, you can take your tax-free cash from a pension fund at 25% of the fund. The balance of the fund can give you an income for life. So, if you are a saver looking for really good returns, you can make a single premium pension contribution every year and immediately take your tax-free cash and an income for life, so long as aged 55+ now. You could have a return of around 25% – 30% per year (depending on your age) if you employ this strategy.

Example

Joe earns £60,000 a year and is age 55. He has no other pension funding. He can contribute up to 100% of relevant earnings, with a maximum of £255,000 in earnings. (Note – special rules for high earners at £150,000 plus per annum could be limited to a £20,000 contribution in this tax year.)

Gross Contribution	£20,000
HMRC uplift at 20%	£4,000

Net contribution by Joe	£16,000
Joe takes 25% tax-free cash (25% x £20,000)	£5,000
Joe gets back a further 20% through tax return	£4,000
(as a higher rate taxpayer, a further 20% is reclaimable)	

Total savings	£9,000
Total cost of investment £16,000 – £9,000 =	£7,000
Balance of fund for income annuity for life	£15,000
giving an estimated monthly income of	£70

Variations

You have a number of choices – you do not need to take tax-free cash immediately – you can let your funds grow to age 75 and then take tax-free cash. You can even take the tax-free cash and defer the income. Very high taxpayers need to be careful on their pension contributions and funding.

Practical tip

If aged over 55 consider the benefits of a personal pension plan as an investment. Your fund grows tax-free, the HMRC adds 20% to every contribution you make and 25% of the whole fund is immediately available to you as tax-free cash. You can take or defer income from the balance of the investment, which would be taxable.'

Dying too soon

The main issue with annuities is that you surrender your capital. In other words, you hand over your entire pension pot on day one -- and your income dies with you. Also, dying young means that you could lose the 'annuity gamble', as your total income could be less than your original investment. In addition, some of your annuity income will form part of your overall taxable income, so extra tax could be due on the yearly payments you receive.

Finally, a retired couple with £14,400 to spare could invest four lots of £3,600 into pensions over the tax years 2010/11 and 2011/2012 using all available allowances. This could secure them tax-efficient income each.

SIPPs and SSAS pension schemes

These pension schemes can hold commercial property (which can be purchased from a connected party). If the property is made over into the pension scheme as a contribution (or series of contributions), then those 'in specie' contributions can be tax relievable to the individual (and also receive the HMRC uplift of 20%).

The asset grows tax-free in the pension scheme. Rental income is received tax-free. When the property is sold by the pension fund, there is no capital gains tax.

On retirement, 25% of the pension fund can come to you as tax-free cash, the balance of the fund must purchase a pension or provide an income.

These types of pension funds can also make loans to an employer at up to 50% of the scheme assets.

Pension schemes can be used for tax-efficient investments. Growth in the pension fund is tax-free. Part of the pension scheme can come back to the investor as tax-free cash. Any pension or annuity though is taxable.

Pension contributions

The pensions financial services sector has probably experienced the most turmoil in the past two years with regard to the introduction and then change of policy as successive Governments serve to limit or restrict not only contributions, but also how much you can fund for. The reason for this is the pension contribution is tax deductible (or uplifted in the first instance by the HMRC by 20% whether a taxpayer or not) if a higher rated or additional rated taxpayer. The fund then grows tax-free. The onslaught by successive Governments on the pensions industry to save taxpayers' money continues unabated. The present position is as follows with regard to making pensions contributions:

Non taxpayers: pay no tax and can contribute up to £3,600 gross, £2,880 net. The HMRC uplifts your contribution by 20%.

Basic rate taxpayers pay tax at 20% on taxable earnings up to £37,400, can contribute up to the lesser of 100% of earnings capped at £255,000 in 2010/11. The cap is £50,000 in 2011/12. The HMRC uplifts your contribution by 20%.

Higher rate taxpayers pay tax at 40% on taxable earnings up to £150,000, can contribute up to the lesser of 100% of earnings capped at £255,000 in 2010/11. The HMRC uplifts your contribution by 20%. There are anti-forestalling provisions for those earning over £130,000, who are limited in 2010/11 to contributions of £20,000 or £30,000 (if already contributing regularly). These taxpayers can claim an additional 20% in tax back from HMRC on their gross contributions. The cap is £50,000 in 2011/12.

Additional rate taxpayers – pay tax at 50% on taxable earnings above £150,000. The above rules for additional rate taxpayers apply for 2010/11, with the addition of taper relief from £150,000 to £180,000 relevant earnings to further reduce claims from HMRC. However, from 2011/12, the maximum pension relief is given at 30% (20% having already been added by HMRC) with a cap of £50,000.

New annual allowance

The new annual allowance for pensions contributions is £50,000 per year from the 2011/12 tax year, which includes all individual and employer contributions. Any unused annual allowance in one tax year can be carried forward the following 3 tax years. You could therefore make a single pension contribution every 4 years of £200,000. Tax relief is given at the highest marginal rate – a 50% taxpayer will get a pension fund of £50,000 for a net cost of £25,000. The LTA – lifetime allowance – for the amount you may fund for pensions, reduces from £1.8 million to £1.5 million in 2012/13. The new £50,000 annual allowance replaces the current annual allowance of £255,000 from April 2011. At the same time, the anti-forestalling measures will cease. The unlimited annual allowance in the last retirement year will be removed from April 2011.

Of interest is that the trivial commutation limit will be de-linked from the lifetime allowance, and will remain at its current level of £18,000 from April 2012. There could be some scope for planners using pensions as investments to take the whole fund in cash if there are no other pension benefits (subject to a part tax charge), without having to purchase an annuity.

Pensions could be the best investment to make, but it is also important to understand pension rules and how these have changed over the years.

Your family home and property investments

The sale of the principal private residence is tax-free.

For most, their home is not seen as an investment, however, for some people it is, and others have second or more homes as investments.

The family home can be a fantastic store of value, for a number of reasons. It can be used to release equity for education fees, or care fees costs, for example.

Taking equity from the family home is tax-free. If loans are required, the re- mortgage interest rates are relatively low and less than person loan rates.

In the past, investors have taken equity from the family home by increasing their mortgages, then invested the proceeds for higher returns. This can be a high risk strategy, and in the past, interest rates on mortgages have shot up and house prices have fallen – often to a negative equity position, and the investor has had to sell his home. The usual risk warnings are given that any loan against your home which is not serviced could end up losing the home.

Many investors prefer bricks and mortar investments and purchase buy to let properties, or second homes. Only your principal private residence is free from capital gains taxes (CGT) when you come to sell it – any second properties may be subject to CGT on gains arising. If selling a second property to avoid CGT applying, you should make it your primary residence for a period before selling it. There are complicated rules that apply, and tax newsletters like Tax Insider consider these and other strategies on a regular basis. There are deductible expenditures available that make your investment into second properties more tax-efficient, and your accountant or tax adviser can discuss these with you.

Parents will try to help their children get on to the property market at some stage, making deposits available to them, or servicing their mortgages or arranging finance for them. This is also the case where a child goes to University and a property is purchased by the parents for the student to manage, which is let to other students. I cover these aspects in my book on School and University Fees Simplified.

Whether the home is an investment or not, there may be inheritance tax implications resulting from home ownership (*see Chapter 12 of Inheritance Tax Simplified which discusses all of these implications*). The family home is usually the one major asset with value that an investor may have. To lose a percentage of it to inheritance taxes at 40% of its value (after the current nil rate band of £325,000), would mean a major asset loss to any family. Whilst you can sell your home tax-free, on death, IHT taxes may become payable, and considerable planning is required to maintain your asset. If IHT is a problem then a strategy could be to reduce the value of the home through taking out equity (or registering loans against it), whilst pursuing IHT efficient investments.

Again risk warnings would apply.

Trading in currencies/FX – spread bets

Taking spread bets is a gamble. You may win some and lose some. Most people lose as this activity is all about market timing and second-guessing the market movements in different currencies. Many investors have been invited to become currency traders, and my email box receives at least one a week. However, beware – I have not met one so far who has consistently made money from this activity. Individuals can do this, or have managers do it for them. Cash is invested into a bank account in the individual's own name. Trades are made from the account. Any profits are free of income tax or capital gains taxes, under the Gaming rules.

These are high risk strategies betting on the movement of indices and currency funds in the main.

Annuities

Non-pension annuities

A lump sum payment can be made into a voluntary purchase (immediate personal or purchased life annuity – PLA) annuity for older people, or more commonly, a temporary annuity, for a pre-determined number of years for any age. Annuity payments can be streamed for regular monthly, quarterly or annual income, part of which is tax-free (as a return of capital), and part of which is taxable.

The interest element of the annuity is taxable, the capital portion is not (20% tax is deducted at source, but higher rates are payable by higher rate taxpayers).

Annuity income is guaranteed for the annuity-paying period, or part of it, depending on what you choose. Annuity income can be level or increasing, so as to combat inflation. You have no access to the annuity capital once the investment is made, and annuity returns have been at a 40-year low, making annuities unattractive to most people. Often annuities are used to fund other investments – in so- called 'back to back' arrangements. If you have impaired health, higher rates may be offered. These annuities are not to be confused with compulsory purchase annuities from pension funds, where all of the income is taxable.

Some annuities are capital protected and a portion of the annuity (sometimes the whole) can be paid to heirs on death of the annuitant.

Immediate Needs annuities – care fees

An immediate care needs annuity is a special purpose annuity used exclusively in the care fees industry. The elderly person is assessed on 5 ADLs (basically these are needs and requirements driven – do you need assistance with washing, eating, mobility, toilet, and other areas such as mental health and cognitive reasoning – and how much do you need), age and life expectancy and other factors. The product provider then provides a quotation for a lump sum to be invested to pay an annuity – a stream of regular income. If paid directly to the care home, *then no tax is paid* on the annuity income. If paid to an individual then the usual annuity rules apply and part of the annuity will be deemed interest and tax payable. The annuity can increase to cater for increasing care fees costs, and is payable for life. It may be also be protected (for an extra charge, or lower rate), so that if you die too soon, your estate can get some capital back.

These annuities can be set up by the person receiving care, by those who hold a power of attorney (such as an EPA – enduring power of attorney or LPA – the more modern lasting power of attorney), or by third parties, such as children for their elderly parents.

An example is a recent client, female, age 87 at the time, and suffering from mild dementia, and with different degrees of ADL requirements. The care fees costs are £2,600 per month escalating at 8% per annum (annuity starting at £10,800 per annum). The cost of the annuity for life was £55,800 and an income stream was provided to complement available pensions and attendant's allowance. If the client survived 4.5 years, then the risk of capital loss shifted to the annuity provider. The return on the investment is 19.8% in the first year, and will increase as the annuity escalates. The client wished to have certainty that she would have enough money to provide for care fees for life, and wished to ring-fence her other assets from care fees costs.

SAYE

Bonuses from savings accounts linked to share-option schemes are tax-free. You do not have to use the funds to purchase the shares, if at the time when the option is exercised, you do not wish to do so.

Zeros

Zeros are part of split capital investment trusts. These are funds that invest in a basket of shares. Trusts may be split into three types of share that are designed to do different things. Income shares get all of the income from dividends, capital shares benefit from any growth but not income and then there are the zeros.

Savers looking to tuck away a set amount are attracted to zeros because they offer attractive returns over five or six years. No income is paid – hence the name zero – and the returns are rolled up and paid at the end, which is why so many people use them to meet school or university fees (although some years ago the investment industry invested in each other's zeros causing illiquidity and a collapse of values which cost people money). Another attraction is that although returns above the yearly allowance of £10,100 are liable to capital gains tax when they are cashed in, because there is no income, there is no income tax due.

Zeros can be particularly attractive for investors who do not generally utilise their annual CGT allowances (£10,100 for 2010/11 tax year), since it will often be possible to obtain the return 'tax-free'.

For a top rate tax payer who does not utilise his CGT allowances, a return of, say, 6% from a zero is the equivalent to a return of 10% from an interest bearing account.

The quality of Zeros varies considerably and this is usually reflected in the yields. The lowest yields are typically offered by Zeros which have a high level of 'cover' and no bank debt or other prior charges. In the case of Zeros which are not fully covered the notional yield may well be hypothetical.

Investors are advised to seek professional independent advice before buying individual Zeros.

The above are the main investments that have a tax-free element, either wholly tax-free or partially tax-free.

6

Tax-Reducing Investments

Tax-reducing investments are those investments that actually reduce tax payable. This could be reducing an actual tax bill or reducing taxable income. The following are the main tax-reducing investments considered:

- Venture Capital Trusts – VCTs
- Enterprise Investment Schemes – EIS
- Enterprise Zone Investments – EZ's
- Pension Fund Contributions

Venture Capital Trusts (VCT)

A VCT is like a big ISA, but is tax deductible. You can invest up to £200,000 per person and 30% of the investment made reduces your tax bill. (You must have a tax bill to reduce). Income from the VCT, including dividends, is tax-free, and no capital gains tax is payable on gains. Subscriptions for new shares in VCTs attract an Income Tax rebate of 30%. However, you can only reclaim tax that you have paid. Tax credits on dividends are NOT reclaimable. The VCT shares must be held for at least five years.

VCTs are quoted limited companies whose purpose is to invest shareholders' funds in smaller unquoted trading companies (including AIM listed stocks) – with potential for growth and to eventually be floated on the stock market, sold, or refinanced – with a view to making a profit in a tax-efficient way.

VCTs are run by investment managers, and raise their funds from private investors. Money raised from individual investors is pooled in order to acquire a portfolio of different investments and to spread the risk. The VCT shares are quoted on the London Stock Exchange.

Higher risk investments

This type of investment is seen as being *higher risk* as a VCT invests into unquoted companies and AIM stocks. However, a number of capital – protected and asset protected VCTs are in existence, which help to reduce the risk. There is no legal minimum investment, but minimum investments described in the prospectus's being offered, tend to range from £3,000 to £10,000.

If you have a large income you might be tempted by the generous tax reliefs to invest the maximum permitted under the rules. It is suggested that the right approach is to consider first how much of your investable assets should be committed to UK smaller companies (probably no more than 25%), then use VCTs to provide part of that exposure.

VCT providers

Octopus, named as 'VCT Provider of the Year' for the past 4 years, has some 15 VCTs under management and over £300 million invested into VCTs alone. Their minimum investment is £3,000 in their new VCT issue Octopus Second Aim VCT. This VCT invests generally into AIM and Plus quoted stocks, and managers have a history of increasing dividend payments and very good returns operating in difficult trading conditions.

Edge Performance VCT 'G' share is raising capital to invest in the entertainments industry and events companies, and offers targeted returns and downside protection – the latter through contractual minimum revenues and capital guarantees from counterparties. The minimum investment is £5,000.

Foresight Solar VCT has a portfolio of UK solar assets, making use of the Government's index-linked guarantee for a minimum price for electricity produced from renewable sources. The minimum investment is £3,000.

The above are three examples of VCTs in different sectors, open for investment.

All offer a tax-free dividend policy to return funds to investors, and risk spreading through investing into a variety of different qualifying companies.

The main VCT investment 'season' is from 1.1.2011 to 5.4.2011, although a number of VCTs are open for investment during the year. Investors should spread their VCT investments amongst different providers for diversification.

Most VCTs aim to give back capital by way of distributions. Best Invest (www.bestinvest.co.uk) and Allanbridge (www.taxshelterreport.co.uk) show current and past VCTs' performance. See how past VCTs have performed. These are also quoted investments and their prices can be found online or in the Financial Times and other newspapers.

Amount to invest

The maximum is £200,000 in any one tax year for tax reliefs to apply. Investments over that amount do not qualify for tax relief. Reinvested dividends count towards the £200,000 limit.

Income tax relief

20% of the amount invested up to £200,000 is deductible from your income tax. There is a maximum income tax deduction of £60,000 (£200,000 x 30%). You must have the tax liability to reduce though.

Example
You invest £100,000.

Tax Payable	£30,000
Less VCT investment of £100,000 at 30%	£30,000

Tax payable	£0

Investment period

The investment must be held for 5 years to maintain the tax relief (it was 3 years to 6 April 2006). If you divide the tax relief of 30% by the 5 year investment term to qualify for income tax reliefs, then this works out as a guaranteed return of 6% p.a. for the five years. Recycling is possible to get the tax reliefs again. However, many VCTs return your funds piecemeal, mainly through dividend declarations, and you are unlikely to have your full original lump sum available for re-investment.

Minimum age

Minimum age to invest is age 18. There is no maximum age.

Capital Gains Tax

Previously (to 2004) the VCT could be used for capital gains tax deferral, however, this is no longer the case.

Dividends

Dividends paid by VCTs are not liable to any tax and any capital gain on selling the shares is not liable to CGT. These 'ISA type' reliefs apply to purchases of existing VCT shares as well as on subscriptions for new shares.

Claiming tax relief

Each VCT will issue a certificate to subscribers, usually within a few weeks of the share allotment. This is used to claim the relief in conjunction with a Self Assessment form. If relief applies for the current tax year, write to your tax inspector and ask for a coding change.

Losses

Investment losses are not tax deductible.

Inheritance tax and death

VCTs are fully listed shares and so treated in the same way as other equities. In other words there are no IHT benefits from investing in VCTs. There are no business property reliefs (BPR) that you may get if you invest directly into an unquoted share or AIM share. Under BPR your share investment would be out of your estate after 2 years (see the EIS section that follows).

Upon death, the whole value of a VCT can pass to a spouse, along with the rest of your estate, and is liable for inheritance tax. However, even if you die before the five year minimum period for Income Tax relief is reached, your estate will not have to repay this tax relief money.

2010 Budget changes

The main changes are:

- VCTs will be able to list their shares in any EU/EEA country. At the moment they can only be listed in the UK.
- VCTs will have to own at least 70% of their investments in companies in eligible shares, up from the current 30%. However, the definition of eligible shares will change to allow VCTs to include shares which may carry certain preferential rights to dividends.

For both EIS and VCT schemes the current requirement that a company must carry on a qualifying trade wholly or mainly in the UK will be replaced with the less onerous condition of simply having a permanent establishment in the UK.

What type of investor is a VCT suitable for?

VCT's are not suitable for all investors. They might be right for your investment portfolio if you:

- Are looking to reduce you income tax liability.
- Seek a long-term investment opportunity.
- Are in a position to take on a higher risk for potentially higher gains.
- Want a highly tax-efficient alternative to other funds that invest in UK smaller companies.
- Are seeking to potentially reduce the overall risk to your investment portfolio with a fund that typically follows a different cycle to stock markets.
- Require an additional source of retirement income (you are not locked in as you are with a pension.) However, the periods of investment at 5 years minimum to retain tax reliefs, may not be long enough, or even too short for you. The investment could also be illiquid, and you do not have a ready market for your shares, when you may need liquidity or cash.
- Are looking for an alternative tax-efficient investment to an ISA. However note that an ISA investment has instant access and can be liquidated if you need cash. A VCT investment is largely illiquid and your capital is tied up for a number of years.

Venture Capital Trust investments will become more popular for higher earners as pension contribution relief becomes more restricted. However, it also has appeal to some higher risk ISA investors who are looking for tax relief on their tax-free investment. At the end of the investment period, you could end up with a tax-free pot of cash. This is distributed to you tax-free.

Enterprise Investment Schemes (EIS)

In order to encourage investment into small businesses, the legislation offers a number of tax reliefs to investors. These are reliefs from income tax and capital gains tax, relief from inheritance tax, and loss reliefs. These reliefs reflect the risky nature of investing into unquoted companies, that may include certain AIM stocks.

Income tax relief

Investing into a qualifying EIS company will be tax deductible at 20% of your investment. Up to £500,000 may be invested per person and 20% of the investment reduces your actual tax bill (you must have a tax bill to be reduced). EIS shares must be held for 3 years to qualify for tax reliefs.

EIS can only be made by individuals for tax reliefs (Trusts can make EIS investments to defer CGT though, but not get income tax reliefs). You do not need to be resident in the UK, you merely need a UK income tax liability to claim the relief.

Example

You have a tax bill of £20,000 and £100,000 to invest

Tax Liability	£20,000
Less EIS investment £100,000 at 20%	£20,000
Tax Liability	£0

The tax deduction can be related back to the previous tax year in full. This is a particularly useful tax strategy as there are not many deductions that can be related back to a previous tax year. You can backdate part or all of your investment into a previous tax year. The full amount of the tax relief can be backdated to a previous tax year. This is a new rule under FA 2009. (Previously it was limited to 50% of the investment made and capped at £10,000 tax relief).

Relief cannot be carried forward to a later year. Tax relief may only be claimed when invested into the company (and not when you invest into a Portfolio or Fund).

Loss reliefs

Losses on EIS shares – you may claim loss relief of the amount invested less any tax relief previously given. This relief is available against income or capital gains.

Note that tax relief cannot be set against dividend income (as the tax credit attached to the dividend is not recoverable).

Dividends

Dividends are taxable.

Capital gains tax deferral relief

You can defer a capital gain indefinitely and it dies with you through investing into an EIS investment. The investment to defer the gain is unlimited (not limited to £500,000) and can be made one year before and up to 3 years after the date of disposal leading to the gain.

However, if in the last 3 years you have paid CGT at 40%, then investing into an EIS to defer CGT will also return the tax paid at 40%. Once the event is crystallised, the investment can be sold (e.g. AIM Shares) and tax paid at 18% or 28%.

Capital gains on disposal are tax-free.

CGT deferral is unlimited (although only £500,000 will qualify for income tax relief).

Individuals and trusts can invest into an EIS qualifying investment to defer a capital gain. Capital gains tax is at 18%-28% for individuals and 28% for trusts, and an EIS investment can be used to defer a capital gain. This means that you do not pay the capital gains tax until you recrystallise the gain. You could do this each year to use your personal allowance, until you have got rid of the gain.

Inheritance tax

EIS shares reduce your estate after two years for IHT purposes.

If the EIS shares are held for 2 years, then the value and growth on those shares falls out of your estate for IHT. The asset backed or capital protected EIS offerings are used more for IHT reduction, as they offer a perceived more secure route for your money. The two year period is from the time the EIS investment was first made. If subsequently that investment is replaced with another, then the EIS clock continues to run – you do not have to start the EIS period again.

Spouse transfers

Transfers of EIS shares can be made between husband and wife/civil partners, and the recipient stands in the shoes of the transferor.

The Investor

There are no age limits to be an EIS investor. However, for contractual reasons, most EIS offerings will be to someone age 18 and older.

This investment is classed as high risk, as it invests into unquoted companies.

Individuals can invest into an EIS qualifying company and also work in the company and receive remuneration as paid directors.

EIS companies – getting paid as an investor

The company

Must have a qualifying trade, for at least 4 months, which can include research and development. There is a list of trades that do not qualify, such as nursing homes, dealing in land or commodities, banking, leasing, property development farming etc.

The company must issue an EIS 3 certificate for the investor's tax relief to be claimed.

Investors

Some investors wish to 'follow' their investments and to be involved in some way with the company invested into and are investors who have a particular expertise to offer a business, and wish to be paid for their involvement. A little known fact is that an investor can retain tax reliefs *and* receive an income from the company. This is usually in the form of director's fees. This is ideal for someone, for example, who invests redundancy money into the company who also needs a job; or a serial investor seeking paid directorships. Your expertise could be in finance, marketing or whatever, for say 2 days a week.

Connecting rules

The general rule is that if an investor is connected with a company, then EIS tax reliefs could be lost or not available. You are connected with the company if you control the company; have more than 30% of the votes; your shares plus loan capital exceed 30% of the share capital plus loan capital; you trade in partnership with the company; you are an employee of the company; you are a director (unless exempted); you subscribe for shares as part of an arrangement where another buys shares where you are connected. *See ICTA/S219A (4) & (5) and ITA/S169 and VCM25080.*

Exemptions

You are *not* treated as connected, if you are an unpaid director; your expenses as a director are reimbursed for performance as a director; you may have interest on funds loaned to the company; reasonable dividends; a reasonable rent for property let to the company; reasonable charges or remuneration for services (not secretarial or managerial) provided to the company. *See ICTA/S291A (3); ITA/S 168(2) & (3) or VCM25070.*

You must not have been a director prior to investing – otherwise you lose your tax reliefs.

Example

Betsy invests £50,000 for 25% of the shares into Salop Marketing, a qualifying EIS company. She receives 20% income tax relief at £10,000.

She provides financial expertise for 3 days a month for £1,500 per month to the company. Including her tax relief, she would have her initial investment returned in just under 3 years. Betsy would not lose her tax reliefs, and stays close to the business, and assists it to be profitable. The director's fees she earns will be taxable in her hands. As an EIS qualifying company, no CGT is payable when she sells her shares.

A number of companies will do this kind of deal. They not only get expertise, but they get investment cash to use for company purposes. This type of deal would not be available if investing through an EIS portfolio or EIS fund.

Investment routes

There are two main routes into making ISA investments – direct EIS investment into a qualifying company or an investment into an EIS Fund or Portfolio. Managers tend to group EIS companies into portfolios to spread risk. EIS remains a very high risk investment as you are investing into unquoted companies and AIM shares.

Some product providers, such as Octopus and Downing have had asset backed or capital protected EIS investments where the capital is under less risk. However, expect next to no return from these types of investments. Your return is the tax relief of 20% (held for 3 years, equates to around 7% p.a. for the 3 years).

A number of companies – such as Octopus with its Eureka EIS Portfolio Service (this has achieved an internal rate of return of over 15% p.a. even including the recent financial crisis), Rathbones, Oxford Capital Partners and others group together EIS companies into a portfolio to reduce risk through spreading the investments. Some EIS portfolio managers have not done well at all – Brewin Dolphin for one with some portfolios lost over 80% of value in recent years, as AIM stocks were particularly hard hit in the recent financial downturn. Previously they had averaged around 16% p.a. It pays to shop around and see how various EIS managers have done in the past (even though past performance is no guide to future returns, it is used as a benchmark by many investors.)

For general legislation and guidance on EIS, see http://www.hmrc.gov.uk/eis/guidance.pdf for further information. There are also finance houses that provide details on companies seeking investment from 'business angels', who will invest their money for equity in the company, and possibly for paid expertise.

However, not all investors are business angels. Some are merely looking to diversify their investment portfolios, or seeking inheritance tax mitigation, or who wish to defer a capital gain.

What type of investor is an EIS suitable for?

EIS's are not suitable for all investors. They might be right for your investment portfolio if you:

- Are looking to reduce you income tax liability.
- Seek a long-term investment opportunity. You must be prepared to invest for at least 3 years to keep the EIS tax reliefs.
- Are in a position to take on a higher risk for potentially higher gains.
- Want a highly tax-efficient alternative to other funds that invest in UK smaller companies.
- Are seeking to potentially reduce the overall risk to your investment portfolio with an investment that typically follows a different cycle to stock markets (private equity).
- Require an additional source of retirement income, or non-executive director (you are not locked in as you are with a pension.) However, the periods of investment at 3 years minimum to retain income tax reliefs, may not be long enough, or even too short for you. The investment would most certainly also be illiquid, and you do not have a ready market for your shares, when you may need liquidity or cash.
- Are looking for an alternative tax-efficient investment to an ISA. However note that an ISA investment has instant access and can be liquidated if you need cash. An EIS investment is largely illiquid and your capital is tied up for a number of years. EIS investments will become more popular for higher earners as pension contribution relief becomes more restricted.

Enterprise Zone investments (EZT or EZ)

Investments into Enterprise Zones carry tax reducing advantages. The investment made (which can be unlimited) gives tax relief by reducing your taxable income, which, in turn, should reduce your tax bill. These are generally bricks and mortar investments into commercial buildings that have been pre-let, which reduces risk.

After 30 years, there is now less than 6 months left for investors to take advantage of Enterprise Zone tax legislation. From 6th April 2011, EZS will no longer be available.

Of the EZ syndicates available, Chancery(UK) LLP are offering investors the choice of investing in a hi-tech data centre in Dunalastair, North Lanarkshire and/or a high quality traditional office in Cobalt Park, Newcastle upon Tyne. These EZ investments enable investors to shelter their higher and additional rate taxable income. There is a non-status, limited recourse loan to facilitate the investment, and an investor cash deposit of £37,500 (37.5%).

On a gross investment of £100,000 the estimated tax relief for a 40% taxpayer is £39,640 (39.6%) and for a 50% taxpayer, £49,550 (49.6%).

EZ investments are now very limited and usually syndicated. The amount invested (by individual or company) reduces taxable income and is usually around 90% of the investment – as land is not deductible, but buildings are through allowances.

Enterprise Zone legislation was created in 1980, so there is a 30 year plus track record for this non tax contentious investment vehicle. An EZ investment is a tax mitigation vehicle and *not* a deferral.

Most EZ investments use limited recourse loans as follows:

A non-status, limited recourse loan would be agreed in principle. This means that for every £100,000 invested the investor will just have to find £37,500 (37.5%). The remaining £62,500 (62.5%) is made up by the loan.

The investor can claim up to 100% income tax relief on the proportion of their investment used for "qualifying expenditure".

If the "qualifying expenditure" on an investment was say 98.95%, which means that on an investment of £100,000, a higher rate tax payer will receive tax relief of £39,400 – 39.4%. This varies according to the qualifying expenditure.

The self employed can offset against their January 31st Payment on Account, employed persons can reclaim their tax after 5th April. You can only offset *current* year's income and not a capital gain.

Example

Taxable Income	£150,000
Less EZ investment of £100,000 of which 98% qualifies:	£98,000

Taxable Income reduces to	£52,000

Unless the Government declares further EZ's in the future, this type of tax reduction investment ends in the 2010/2011 tax year.

Pension contributions

A pension contribution in the first instance increases the amount of the basic tax rate band (as opposed to giving a tax deduction) by 20%. Relief is given for higher and additional rated taxpayers at 20%-30% of the gross pension contribution.

Pension contributions can be made of £3,600 gross (£2,880 net) for those without qualifying income, the HMRC adding a further £720. This applies for a grandchild to a non-working spouse or partner.

Contributions may be made up to 100% of earnings, capped at £255,000 in the 2010/11 tax year.

Pension contributions made could offset against realised life policy gains or capital gains in the 2010/11 tax year.

Salary sacrifice, if an employee, could be made to create tax and NI savings that can be added to pension contributions to increase their pension funding.

Pension funds grow tax-free. On retirement, 25% of the fund can be taken as tax-free cash, the balance either pays a taxable annuity or taxable income drawdown.

There have been changes to how pension contributions are made, and the previous and latest positions are given below.

Previous position

Note in the Finance Act 2009, there was particular impact for pensions.

Higher rate tax relief has been restricted for those earning above £150,000 (all income). This is a wider definition than just pensionable earnings. From April 2011 if income is above £180,000 you will only receive tax relief at the basic rate of 20% on pension contributions. This is tapered from £150,000 at 40% to 20% at £180,000 and beyond.

If contributing more than £20,000 and earning over £150,000 in 2010/11 you can still get full tax relief.

Anti-forestalling provisions: from 22nd April 2009 if relevant income £150,000 + in current tax year and two previous tax years, and you change normal ongoing regular pension contributions and if total pension savings exceed £20,000 p.a. – you are restricted (applies only in 2009/10 and 2010/11 tax years to stop excessive pension contributions at reliefs of 40% and 50%.)

There is a proviso to go to £30,000 ('irregular mean') pension contributions if these are not made regularly.

Relevant income includes total income from all sources (includes rental, investment, pension income, any salary sacrifice after 22nd April 2009) and is calculated after normal deductions and reliefs, such as trading losses, pension contributions up to £20,000 and gift aid.

If you make regular contributions (irrespective of size), this remains unchanged, and is not affected.

If contributions (employer and employee) do not exceed £20,000, you are not affected.

If contributions are greater than £20,000, but income over this year and the last 2 years is below £150,000 – not affected.

Latest position

Non taxpayers: pay no tax and can contribute up to £3,600 gross, £2,880 net. The HMRC uplifts your contribution by 20%.

Basic rate taxpayers pay tax at 20% on taxable earnings up to £37,400, can contribute up to the lesser of 100% of earnings capped at £255,000 in 2010/11. The cap drops to £50,000 in 2011/12. The HMRC uplifts your contribution by 20%.

Higher rate taxpayers pay tax at 40% on taxable earnings up to £150,000, can contribute up to the lesser of 100% of earnings capped at £255,000 in 2010/11. The HMRC uplifts your contribution by 20%. There are anti-forestalling provisions for those earning over £130,000, who are limited in 2010/11 to contributions of £20,000 or £30,000 (if already contributing regularly). These taxpayers can claim an additional 20% in tax back from HMRC on their gross contributions. The cap is £50,000 in 2011/12.

Additional rate taxpayers –pay tax at 50% on taxable earnings above £150,000. The above rules for additional rate taxpayers apply for 2010/11, with the addition of taper relief from £150,000 to £180,000 relevant earnings to further reduce claims from HMRC. However, from 2011/12, the maximum pension relief is given at 30% (20% having already been added by HMRC) with a cap of £50,000.

In the future, any unused annual pension allowance can be carried forward for 3 years – you could therefore make a contribution of £200,000 (for the carry forward and that current year's contribution). Note, though that the lifetime allowance (LTA) has been reduced to £1.5 million from £1.8 million in 2011/12.

Reducing taxable income

Most advisers will consider whether total taxable income can be reduced through tax reducing investments to a level below £150,000. For example EZ investments reduce taxable income. The problem is that the anti-forestalling provisions cover the last two tax years and the current one, and the only tax-reducing investment that relates tax reduction back to the previous tax year is EIS investments. That reduces tax but not taxable income. Film partnership investments used to go back up to 3 years, but those investments are no longer available.

Personal Allowances reduced from 6.4.2010 for earnings of £100,000 or more. The personal allowance will taper to zero at £112,950. The marginal rate of tax where the personal allowance is lost will be 60%.

Example – restricted personal allowance and pension contributions

Income	£114,000	Allowance	£6,475
Pension Contribution	£5,000		

	£109,000		
Limit	£100,000		

Excess	£9,000	Restrict ½	£4,500

		Allow	£1,975
Income	£114,000		
Limited Allowance	£1,975		

Chargeable	£112,025		
Tax Payable	£37,400 x 20% =	£7,480.00	
	£74,625 x 40% =	£29,850.00	

Tax due		**£37,330.00**	

Making pension contributions can reduce taxable income to enable more of your personal allowance to be effective.

To show the effect of increased marginal rates of tax with the loss of the personal allowance, consider the following example with 50% income tax rate at £150,000 (42.5% tax rate on dividends if earning £150,000+) and no personal allowance:

Example

If income is £170,000 in 2010/11

Tax is: 20% x £37,400	£7,480
40% x £112,600	£45,040
50% x £20,000	£10,000

Total	£62,520

Marginal rates of tax are then:

£100,000 to £112,950	– 60% effective rate
£112,951 – £149,999	– 40% effective rate
£150,000 +	– 50% effective rate

Pension contributions can reduce tax paid, as can other tax-reducing investments. Making a pension contribution reduces taxable income, and a pension contribution could reduce taxable income sufficiently to perhaps fall out of the personal allowance trap.

7

Taxable But Still Efficient

Investments can be made that are taxable, but because of personal allowances, could still be tax-efficient. The main personal allowances are those for taxable income, which are dependent on age, and capital gains tax allowances, as well as allowances for inheritance tax.

Personal Allowances

You may have taxable investments, however your personal allowances would render all or part of them tax-free. Personal Allowances for 2010/11 are as follows:

Under age 65:	£6,475
65 -74	£9,490
75 and over:	£9,640

These increase by £1,000 in the 2011/12 tax year.

Age related allowances are progressively withdrawn if taxable income exceeds £22,900 if over age 65.

From 6.4.2010, the personal allowance which is restricted for individuals with a net adjusted income of £100,000+ tapers to nil, and the effective tax rate becomes 60% between £100,000 and £112,950. There is therefore a great need for tax planning to reduce taxable income sufficiently so that it is below £100,000, where possible.

You may have taxable income and expect this to be reduced by the personal allowance, however, if the level of taxable income is above £100,000, then you lose your personal allowance progressively until you reach £112,950. Your strategy may be to reduce taxable income with an EZ investment, and/or pension contributions, or other deductions allowable, if you are self-employed for example.

Capital Gains Tax allowance

The CGT allowance is £10,100 per person in the 2010/11 tax year. A couple would have £20,200 worth of capital gains tax allowances between them. Trusts have an exemption of £5,050 per trust, divided up to 5 trusts.

Gains (growth) can be taken free of taxes at up to this personal allowance amount. Check investments for capital gains and possibly dispose of enough to satisfy this allowance. Some growth investments where the gains can be taken, can be used to provide annual income in this way.

Capital Gains are taxed at rates of 18% or 28%, depending on your income.

Taxable investments

The main investments that are taxable are given below (note this may not cover every investment opportunity).

- American life Settlements
- Bank and Building Society Savings and deposit accounts
- Corporate Bonds
- ETFs
- Gilts
- Investment trusts
- OEICS
- Shares
- Structured investments
- Traded Endowment Policies
- Unit Trusts

American Life Settlements investments

Many see this as a new asset class. One can invest usually through Life Settlements Funds. These can provide growth or income.

The fund or trust purchases a whole of life policy from an individual in the USA who has been diagnosed with a terminal illness, and is aged late 70's to 80's. Two independent medical assessors assess the life expectancy of the individual, which may be 6 months, 1 year or longer. An offer is made to purchase the policy at a discount to the face value (sum assured). Assume that the policy is $1 million sum assured with Prudential. It is purchased for $500,000. The fund takes over the payment of the premiums. On death, $1 million pays out to the fund. The gain made is not subject to stock market movements or interest rates, and is said to be non-correlated. Roughly 77% of people die on time, others die early, and some late.

How safe is this investment? There have been occasions where fraud has occurred on a fund (Keydata) and SLS Capital, as well as earlier examples, such as Mutual Benefits. However, the industry is well established, and many funds show excellent track records.

A new development has been the USA taxing benefits (previously regarded as tax-free to the fund), and fund managers have sought to find tax havens for their products. Another issue has been distributor or non distributor status of funds. Most funds maturities or payouts to investors have been from non-distributor fund status, and subject to income tax. Some funds have distributor status, which would be subject to capital gains tax.

On the aspect of non-correlation, whilst the product itself may be non-correlated, the credit crunch has shown that pricing of products has been affected due to supply and demand factors, and that the fund values have been written down (net asset values), and some funds have even been suspended for a period, such as the Life Settlements Fund – an Australian unit trust and the largest fund of its kind in the world – to stop early redemptions. There was therefore some correlation with falling investment markets, and these funds could not be said to be uncorrelated.

Bank and building society savings and deposit accounts

The interest on bank and building society savings accounts is taxable.

HMRC automatically takes 20% of your savings interest 'at source' – before you receive it. So, if you're a non-taxpayer or only pay tax at 10%, then you could be paying too much tax. Get a form R40 from the taxman and claim what's owed – you can go back as far as 2004/05. In addition, fill in a form R85 at your bank or building society to stop future overpayments. This would save three million people with low earnings a total of £330 million a year.

Bank and building society savers accounts currently pay negligible interest on current accounts. Interest payments increase generally the longer you hold the account. The best savings accounts are term deposit accounts, which are available both onshore in the UK and offshore in tax haven jurisdictions, such as the Isle of Man, Jersey or Guernsey and elsewhere. An indication of saver's rates can be found in the financial pages of newspapers, or by visiting the FSA website at www.moneymadeclear.org.uk or any of the recognised websites such as www.thisismoney.co.uk, www.moneysupermarket.com, www.moneyfacts.co.uk and others.

A 5 year fixed rate savings account is currently offering 4.6% with interest payable annually. A 4 year fixed rate savings account pays 4.20%, a 3 year one pays 3.85%, 2 year one pays 3.5% and 1 year interest is at 3%. All have interest payable annually, and all are onshore. Offshore rates are slightly higher.

Some savings accounts offer a higher rate, but this includes a 'bonus' if you stick with the term.

The absolute worst rates pay 0% or 0.1%, and some big names players are in this category, like Santander and HSBC.

Interest is subject to income tax. Low levels of savings interest could be taxed at 10% up to £2,440, thereafter at 20% (but the 10% tax rate is only available if taxable non savings income exceeds the starting rate band of £2,440.

The basic personal allowance of £6,475 gives you this amount of taxable interest tax-free.

Corporate bonds

A corporate bond is an investment offered by companies, UK and foreign national, public or local authorities, where these bodies borrow money. They must be qualifying corporate bonds denominated in sterling and be fixed interest, non-convertible loans. There is no age limit and no capital gains tax is payable, however, interest is subject to income tax and basic tax rate is deducted at source. There is no maximum limit, and the minimum is around £2,000. The corporate bond pays a fixed rate of interest over the life of the bond, which is certain and known at the time of issue of the bond. You can realise a capital gain if you dispose of the bond or receive income if you hold it. Bonds are usually sold at a discount, and the price is fixed by the term to redemption and the underlying level of interest rates. Bonds are categorised as convertibles (can convert to ordinary shares of the issuing company), zero coupon bonds (pay little or no interest), local authority bonds (issued with a guaranteed rate of one year and six days, with rates of interest fixed at the outset, or for 3-4 years. Issued at par there are no capital gains. Eurobonds are flexible foreign currency bonds with fixed or variable interest and may have a currency risk and yield risk from non sterling currencies.

Interest is subject to income tax and is paid net of lower rate tax. Non-taxpayers can reclaim basic rate tax at source. Basic rate taxpayers pay tax at 20%. Higher rate taxpayers pay tax at 40% or 50%. There is no CGT on gains when sold, and any losses are not offset for capital gains tax. The above applies to qualifying corporate bonds. If the bond is non-qualifying, then such bonds are subject to CGT.

Exchange Traded Funds (ETFs)

These are traded like normal shares, ETFs allow you to spread your investments across a wide range of securities, thus tracking the performance of an entire index, but within a single share. They are becoming more popular as investments and used by financial planners and portfolio builders.

Because it trades like a share, an ETF does not have its net asset value (NAV) calculated every day like a mutual fund (unit trust) does. With the opportunity to spread your risk across an entire index, ETFs are an ideal building block for a balanced portfolio. This brings real power – helping you to track share and bond markets and make strategic investments easier and more cost-effective. Exchange Traded Funds (ETFs) give investors the chance to buy whole indices as easily as buying a share on the London Stock Exchange. Eligible for inclusion in ISAs but attracting no stamp duty, ETFs have the lowest annual charges of all collective investment schemes. An ETF is an investment fund traded on stock exchanges, much like shares. An ETF holds assets such as shares, commodities, or bonds and trades at approximately the same price as the net asset value of its underlying assets over the course of the trading day. Most ETFs track an index, such as the

FTSE 100, and may be attractive as investments because of their low costs, tax efficiency, and share-like features.

In essence, an ETF is a hybrid of a share and a pooled index fund. It provides instant diversification like a fund by tracking an index. Performance of ETFs closely matches the performance of the relevant underlying index. Clearing and settlement of ETFs is just like any other share. Dividends accumulate and are paid out at regular intervals. Management fees are deducted directly from the dividend yield. At present ETFs do not incur stamp duty. ETFs can only be bought and sold through any stockbroker. ETFs are simple low cost, diversified investments with no hidden charges. Like shares, any gains are subject to capital gains tax and dividends are taxed according to your marginal rates of tax for dividends.

Gilts

Gilts are known as Government Fixed Interest Stock. A gilt represents Government borrowing and is initially issued at a discount to its redemption value, over a number of years, prior to being redeemed at par (face value). It enables investors to plan for known future investments, such as education fees or care home fees.

Gilts are UK Government securities issued by HM Treasury. Since April 1998 gilts have been issued by the DMO (Debt Management Office) on behalf of HM Treasury. The DMO took over gilt issuance from the Bank of England, following the transfer of responsibility for setting interest rates from HM Treasury to the Bank in May 1997. Gilts may be conventional or index-linked.

Interest received is taxable and must be declared on tax returns. This includes the interest uplift on index-linked gilts. But the uplift in principal as a result of index-linking is not interest, and is not taxable.

A fixed rate of interest is payable over the life of the gilt. The interest rate is known as the annual percentage rate on £100 nominal stock. This is known as the coupon. The yield on the stock is dependent on the price of £100 when you make the purchase. Repayment of the nominal value of the stock is guaranteed on the redemption date. Stocks are usually issued as a discount to its redemption price of £100. The less the term to redemption, the more the price of the stock will rise. Gilt prices rise and fall on a daily basis, according to interest rate activity and other factors. The following commentary, to show the effect of rises and falls, taken from a market commentator on Bloomberg news, 29th October 2010:

Gilts Rise

Government bonds rose, with the 10-year gilt yield falling seven basis points to 3.08 percent. The 4.75 percent security due March 2020 rose 0.57, or 5.7 pounds per 1,000-pound ($1,599) face amount, to 113.48. The two-year yield fell four basis points, to 0.67 percent.

The 10-year gilt yield has climbed 13 basis points this week. It rose to 3.19 percent on Oct. 27, the highest level since Aug. 11, according to Bloomberg generic data. The two-year note yield has gained three basis points this week.

Gilts returned investors 7.8 percent since the end of 2009, beating a 7.7 percent gain from German debt, but less than the 8.4 percent return from U.S. Treasuries, according to indexes compiled by Bloomberg and the European Federation of Financial Analysts Societies.

The Government issues gilts, also known as gilt-edged securities, to fund its borrowing – in effect when you buy gilts you are lending the Government money. Issued in £100 units, they promise to pay a fixed income over a fixed term. Investors are repaid the nominal capital value when the gilt matures.

There are different types of gilt. Some run only for a few years, while others last for up to 30 years. There are index-linked gilts, meaning that interest and capital payments are adjusted to take inflation into account. Others are "strippable", which means that the individual interest and redemption payments may be bought and sold separately. The most common category is the conventional gilt.

Financial advisers believe that gilts have a place as part of a balanced portfolio, although their risk status does mean that returns are very low. Older people can use them as a core holding around which to add other investments that carry higher risk.

The amount of income you get, and for how long you get it, is in the title of the gilt you buy. Take a conventional gilt, for example, and a holding of £1,000 nominal of 4.75% Treasury Stock 2020. If you purchase £1,000 nominal of 4.75% Treasury Stock 2010 you will get £47.50 income a year until 2010, plus you will get back £1,000 when the gilt matures.

The £1,000 nominal is the amount of the gilt. It is not necessarily how much it is worth, or how much it cost you to buy. A £1,000 nominal holding of that gilt may be worth more or less than £1,000 in the market. But when this gilt matures you will get back £1,000 in 2020.

The 4.75% coupon amount is the income you will receive each year. Dividends are usually paid twice a year.

The price of the gilt will depend on how attractive the 4.75% coupon is at that time. With savers interest rates at 3%, a 4.75% return looks attractive and so the price will be higher than the £1,000 nominal value. However, if interest rates were 6%, the coupon of 4.75% would look unattractive and so the price would fall below £1,000.

Interest and repayment are guaranteed by the Government. The minimum investment is £1,000 and the maximum £250,000.

Capital gains are free of capital gains tax (but losses are not relievable). Interest can be paid gross (non residents in the UK may receive tax-free interest on certain issues). Interest is liable to income tax at basic, higher and additional rates and is taxed as savings income. There is no stamp duty on the purchase or sale of Gilts.

If interest rates rise, then capital can decrease.

Investment trusts

An investment trust is represented by shares of a public company. The investor buys shares in the investment trust company which purchases a portfolio of shares in other companies. The investor usually buys these shares at a discount below the net asset value per share – this provides additional value compared to buying directly into shares or unit trusts. Investment trusts can borrow money (known as 'gearing') to purchase shares, thus possibly increasing performance – however it could go the other way and gearing costs could depress performance in falling markets. Some investment trusts are income-producing, others go for capital appreciation, and split-level trusts have income for one class of shares and capital gains for another class. For example, 'zeros' produce no income but have a rate of return which is pre-determined when the trust is wound up.

The amount of shares in issue is exactly known, making the investment trust 'closed ended'. This is compared to a unit trust, where the units represent an 'open-ended' fund, making it more susceptible to funds flowing in and out.

Investment trusts can be approved or unapproved. Approved investment trusts are exempt from capital gains within the trust, and dividends are reinvested in full. This is not the case with unapproved investment trusts where a double charge to CGT can arise.

The investment trust pays around 30% tax on unfranked income, but not on dividends from UK companies (unfranked income).

For the investor, capital gains are taxable (less the personal allowance) when the shares are sold by the investor, and dividends received from the investment trust are subject to deduction of lower rate tax at source. Dividends payable come with a tax credit equal to 1/9th of the cash amount. The grossed up dividend is deemed to be the highest part of income, and the tax credit offsets the tax payable. If a non taxpayer, the tax credit is not recoverable.

There are no investment limits, and if age under 18 you cannot hold shares in your own name.

Open-Ended Investment Companies (OEICs)

The OEIC is a hybrid of an investment trust and a unit trust. The OEIC is able to issue shares, but these are open-ended, like a unit trust. The Oeic manager can issue different classes of shares and these are single-priced, unlike a unit trust which has a bid-offer spread. OEICS may set up umbrella funds where investors can choose a fund and make switches later between different asset classes.

There is no capital gains tax within the fund, but an individual investor may suffer CGT when switching funds or selling shares. Dividends received are taxed in the normal way, and a tax credit reduces the dividend tax payable.

The OEIC itself pays tax on a rate similar to the savings rate of 20%, and receive relief for their management expenses and interest paid. Franked income, such as UK dividends, does not suffer further tax; interest and unfranked income suffer tax at 30%, after deducting allowable expenses.

There is no minimum age, and risk is managed and reduced by investment spread. Investments can be made monthly or by lump sum. The minimum lump sum investment for some providers is £500.

Shares

You must be age 18 and above to hold shares/equities. Equities offer potential for growth in capital values and investment income. If shares are sold, you may be liable to capital gains tax above your personal exemption of £10,100 (in 2010/11). Dividends received from shares are grossed up by a tax credit equal to 1/9th of the cash amount (for example, if you receive a dividend of £90, this is grossed up by £10 to a taxable dividend of £100.) The tax credit is offset against the tax liability on the dividend, so that basic rate taxpayers pay no tax, higher rate taxpayers pay effective tax of 22.5%, additional rate taxpayers pay effective tax of 32.5%.

Dividend taxation is at 10% and 32.5%, and 42.5%. Basic rate and non taxpayers pay no further tax; higher rate taxpayers pay a further 22.5%, additional rate taxpayers 32.5%).

Rates at which different dividend tax is payable.

Note that this is the rate before the 10% tax credit applies. For some investments, the tax credit is not repayable.

	On first £2,440	Next £34,960	Next £112,600	Above £150,000
Dividends	10%	10%	32.5%	42.5%

Some qualifying shares (such as some AIM listed or unquoted companies) have IHT advantages, and will be out of your estate after two years and free of inheritance tax.

Permanent interest-bearing shares (PIBS)

PIBS are building society shares listed on the stock exchange (but PIBS are like corporate bonds). These shares increase the capital of the building society and cannot be redeemed, unless the building society is wound up. PIBS offer a high income to investors, but the capital could be at risk. There is no age minimum, the interest payments are fixed, and the yield is generally higher than government stocks. PIBS can be traded to realise capital gains (no CGT is payable), pay interest twice yearly, and have no fixed redemption date. The building society could decide not to pay the interest, and if it does so, this is non-cumulative. Interest is paid gross and subject to tax in the usual way.

Structured investments

These are also known as guaranteed investment products. The usual caveats about 'guarantees' should apply. The bottom line is that the investor is offered a set return some 4-6 years hence, beating bank and building society interest rates. Investment performance is guaranteed over a set term. These products aim to eliminate risk or to guarantee a given return from equity investment. If the stock market used as an index fails to perform over a given period, then the minimum guarantee clicks in (which is usually a return of your capital at various percentages, ranging from 100% down to 50%). So, you get a chance for a capital gain in a rising stock market, and a minimum amount of capital returned. If it does perform appropriately, then you receive your income (if on an income plan) and any additional growth offered. The investment can pay income on a regular basis or a maturity capital gain.

The product provider will usually purchase fixed interest securities, such as certificates of deposit (CDs), and the interest on these is used to buy call options, for the performance element, exercised if the index rises. If it does not, they are not exercised.

For clients who wish to receive a defined return on potential annual increases in the FTSE 100 Index, with a very low risk to capital, Providers (usually banks, such as Barclays, Santander (Cater Allen), Investec and others, offer a capital guarantee and the opportunity to lock-in a return each year that the FTSE 100 Index level is at or above the Initial Index Level.

Example

An example could look like this:

4 year term, the Plan will lock-in a return of 4.25% of your original investment at each averaging period if at that time the FTSE 100 Index level is at or above the Initial Index Level. If, at the end of the term no returns have been locked-in, you will receive your original investment plus a minimum 0.25% return on that investment, or a

6 year term, the Plan will lock-in a return of 5% of your original investment at the end of each averaging period if, at that time, the FTSE 100 Index level is at or above the initial Index Level. If, at the end of the term no returns have been locked-in, you will receive your original investment plus a minimum 0.5% return on that investment.

Please remember, there is no guarantee that the FTSE 100 Index will rise or behave the way it has done in the past.

Gains from returns may be offset against an individual's CGT allowance, or within a SIPP, SSAS, or ISA. It is also available for limited companies, trusts and charities to invest in. Minimum investment is £10,000.

Other providers have different fund types, some offering yields of up to 8% and no initial charges.

These investments are highly sophisticated and also complex. They do entice investors by offering the prospect of stock market growth and guaranteed returns, with or without income, and the investor must be wary. Financial planners need to complete training and be signed off before advising on these products.

Any income received is taxable, and any capital gains are subject to capital gains tax, if UK based, but if in an offshore bond may be subject to income tax.

Traded endowment policies (TEPs)

A traded endowment policy is a second hand policy (mostly with profits policies), that an investor has purchased from the original owner, either directly, or at auction. Instead of surrendering the policy, the original owner may make a small amount over the surrender value by selling it. The new owner takes over the paying of the premiums and receives the maturity proceeds, even if there is a payout on death of the original owner. For the seller as original owner, so long as the policy is a qualifying policy, there should be no tax implications. However, when the investor who has bought the policy either sells it on or receives matured proceeds from it, then these are subject to capital gains tax, if over the personal allowance of £10,100 in 2010/11. If buying these policies, purchase them jointly with your partner for two future CGT personal allowances.

For **qualifying policies**, the gain is calculated as the maturity proceeds less the purchase price and premiums paid.

If the policy is *non-qualifying*, any gains could be subject to income tax with top slicing rules applying. The gain is the maturity proceeds less premiums paid from inception. Basic rate taxpayers pay no further tax; higher rate and additional rate taxpayers pay tax at the difference between the basic tax rate and the individual's tax rate. Capital gains tax could also apply, calculated in the normal way, but also deducting the gain charged to income tax.

Unit trusts

A unit trust is an investment vehicle (there are over 3,000 unit trusts available) where units are purchased by investors, or sold by them for capital gains. The unit trust (also known as mutual funds) industry is well-developed and is able a range of different styled funds to invest into. These range from thematic funds (investing in certain industries or products such as gold) to income funds, or growth funds, or a mix of both, which may be UK based or more geographical. Units are purchased on a bid-offer basis. The price is based on the value of the asset base invested into by the unit trust managers. Incoming money creates more units. When units are sold back to the managers, there are less units reflecting the value of the trust. There are different prices for buying units (bid price) and usually a lower price (offer price) if buying and selling on the same day. Investments may be made monthly or by lump sum and are unlimited. There are no age restrictions.

Capital gains tax arises when units are sold by the investor, and CGT is paid (after taking off your personal allowance of £10,100 in 2010/11) at 18%-28% depending on your marginal rates of tax. Dividends paid come with a tax credit, which is offset against dividend taxation. In the hierarchy of what is taxed first for the taxpayer, dividends grossed up are deemed to be the highest part of income, followed by other savings income, and then earnings. The tax credit is set off against the tax liability of the dividend to reduce the liability to nil for basic rate taxpayers, to 22.5% for higher rated taxpayers and 32.5% for additional rated taxpayers.

8

Tax-Deferred Investments

Investments may be taxable, but the tax can be legally deferred. The following are examples of tax deferral. By not paying the tax now, the investor has the opportunity to allow funds or investments to grow unfettered. However, the tax will have to be paid at some time, unless it dies with you, for example with a capital gains tax deferral.

Investment bonds

These are single premium life assurance policies invested into a wide range of funds and asset allocation classes as selected by you. Each year, the investor could withdraw 5% of the investment 'tax deferred'. These 5%'s are cumulative, so if you don't withdraw anything for, say, 10 years, then you can take 50% out of the bond without any tax charge at that time (10 x 5% = 50%). This is a tax-efficient way of producing an 'income' (return of capital). These withdrawals can be monthly, quarterly or annual. This occurs through periodic part surrenders of the investment bond. The investment purchases a number of segments in the bond, each with an equal value. The investments are either in life assurance or unit linked funds, and the investor has a choice of funds and investment sectors. For larger investments, it is possible to have a discretionary fund manager manage your funds for you.

Investment bonds are available as an onshore investment, or as an offshore investment.

The tax treatment is different, depending on the type of investment selected.

Charges are typically 5% of the investment plus a 1% management fee – however this is negotiable with most product providers.

The minimum investment can be as low as £5,000, but most providers average a minimum of £25,000.

Onshore investment bonds

Tax deferred means that if you are a basic rate taxpayer at maturity of the bond, no further tax is payable – if a higher rate or additional rate taxpayer, income tax as an additional 20%- 30% amount of tax. However, a relief known as 'top slicing' is available to reduce the tax paid. The investment bond policy is not subject to capital gains tax, but to income tax – there is no CGT liability for the investor at maturity.

Onshore investment bonds are suitable for higher rate taxpayers who will become basic rate taxpayers in the future, and for discretionary trusts.

There is no tax charge for basic rate taxpayers on withdrawals made when the tax calculation is made at maturity or a chargeable event.

The life funds are subject to tax on income and capital gains annually. The savings income within the life company's fund is taxed at 20%, and capital; gains are taxed at 20% (or not taxed where linked to returns from Government securities).

Higher and additional rate taxpayers can defer the charge to tax for 20 years if they withdraw no more than 5% per annum for 20 years, of their original investment. If they withdraw more than 5% in any one year, then income tax is payable on the difference between higher/additional rate and basic rate (even if no gain or loss) – this difference is 20% for higher rate taxpayers and 30% for additional rate taxpayers. On the eventual maturity of the investment bond, when say 100% of the original investment has been withdrawn, or the death of the life assured, assignment for money's worth, or encashment of the bond, a tax calculation is made. Additional relief is given to higher/additional rate taxpayers called top slicing relief. It is better to surrender a number of policies than to have a withdrawal across all policies for tax reasons.

Top slicing relief applies and can save tax when the addition of the chargeable gain to the investor's income takes the income across an income tax threshold into a higher rate band. This gain is divided by the number of relevant years to produce an average yearly gain, which is treated as the top slice of income in the tax year in which the gain falls. The tax payable on the top slice is calculated and multiplied by the number of relevant years to give the total income tax payable. For offshore bonds, the top slice is taxed at the taxpayer's highest marginal rate of income tax, but does not benefit from the tax credit applicable to onshore bonds.

Example

Laura has taxable income from employment in the 2010/11 tax year of £36,500 after personal allowances. She has encashed her investment bond after holding it for 7 years, and received a chargeable event gain on the surrender of the policy for £28,500. For 2010/11 higher rate tax applies when taxable income exceeds £37,400.

Computations: as the chargeable event is a full surrender, the number of complete years is 7. Laura's total income, including the chargeable event gain is £65,000. This income falls into the various tax bands as follows:

Tax rate	Amount of total income	Tax chargeable
10%	Not applicable	
20%	£37,400	£7,480
40%	£27,600	£11,040
Total	£65,000	£18,520

The amount of the gain falling within the higher tax rate is £27,600. The rate of additional tax on this amount is 20% (40-20%). The additional tax is then £27,600 x 20% = £5,520.

The 'annual equivalent' of the gain is £4,071 (that is, £28,500/7) and £3,171 of this amount would fall in the higher rate band. This is because if her income of £36,500 is added to the top slice of the gain of £4,071 = £40,571 less the basic rate band of £37,400 = £3,171, which is still within the basic rate tax band of £37,400. The additional tax is £3,171 x 20% = £634.20. Multiplying by 7 gives £4,439.

The amount of top slicing relief is £5,520 − £4,439 = £1,081, which is given in terms of tax against Laura's total tax liability for the year.

Her total tax liability is £18,520 − £1,081 =£17,439.

If Laura's investment bond policy is onshore (a UK insurer) then tax treated as paid is £28,500 x 20% = £5,700 and that reduces her overall liability to £17,439 − £5,700= £11,739.

If this was an offshore bond, then no tax is treated as paid and her overall tax liability remains at £17,439.

Offshore investment bonds

Investment bonds have a wide choice of funds and investments and you can be conservative or adventurous as you please; you can switch investments within the bond, as your circumstances change. You can invest into insured funds, collectives, and investment portfolio, within the insurance contract. The assets of the investment are held by an insurance company based offshore, in Isle of Man, Guernsey, Dublin, Luxembourg or other 'tax havens'.

Unlike an onshore bond, where there is no minimum age, the minimum age is 18 for an offshore bond. Charges are often said to be higher than onshore bonds, but these are negotiable.

Tax treatment of investments

When investments are held in an offshore bond, the tax treatment is the same as that of a UK pension fund. UK dividends are collected net of a non-reclaimable 10% tax credit and interest and capital gains are tax-free. This is known as gross roll-up. There is no income tax liability until the bond is encashed, surrendered or matures. There is no capital gains tax liability for the investor. No tax is payable if the investor is non resident when the investment bond matures, subject to the criteria applying.

Tax and the investor

Tax is deferred for the UK investor. This enables the underlying assets to grow at a faster pace than if they were taxed, and the investor may withdraw up to 5% tax deferred withdrawals.

The policyholder can claim top slicing relief. This reduces the tax bill for lower rate taxpayers where a policy gain takes them into a higher rate of tax.

(See the example for onshore bonds). However, no tax is treated is paid, and the overall tax liability will be treated as the individual's without any deduction for tax paid in the bond fund (as none will have been paid).

There are other tax advantages for investing into an investment bond – some are used to reduce immediate inheritance tax in your estate through a discounted gift trust (this may be appropriate for parents or grandparents). Offshore investment bonds have 'gross roll up' meaning the investments in the bond are not taxed during the growth period. There is no capital gains tax to pay at any time. At surrender or maturity, income tax may be payable, depending on your tax status and residency in the UK or not. However, always compare investment bonds (income taxed) with unit trusts and OEICs which are subject to a much lower capital gains tax.

The bond on encashment is subject to income tax.

With trust taxation at 40% and rising to 50% in 2011, more use should be made of bond wrappers. However ensure that the trust can appoint capital to beneficiaries.

Compared to other investments

For UK resident taxpayers liable to standard UK income tax, investments into unit trusts and OEICs would be more tax-efficient where gains arising are subject to CGT at 18%- 28%, plus one has a CGT exemption of £10,100 in 2010/11. Income from collective investment funds are taxed at your marginal rate or dividend rate applying. Much will depend on the growth of the underlying investment though. One should always compare the different investment types and choices before investing. Investment bonds are subject to income tax in the hands of the investor, whilst income or interest from unit trusts are subject to income tax, dividends to dividend taxation and capital gains tax on any taxable gains.

Encashment and personal allowances

Bond encashment can cause severe taxation problems, particularly in the from 2010/11 tax year, where personal tax reliefs are lost at income over £100,000 and the new 50% tax rate applies to income over £150,000.

One must differentiate between withdrawals and surrenders. The tax treatment could be penal if the wrong actions are taken.

With a withdrawal, a liability to tax arises even though there has not been a gain. Withdrawals taken by partial withdrawal across all policies are liable to UK tax after deducting the 5% accumulative allowance. Tax is treated at the end of the policy year (not the tax year). Withdrawals taken now could be taxed in 2011/12. Where your taxable income plus the withdrawals take you to a threshold over £100,000, then the marginal rate of tax is at 60% between £100,000 and £112,950 as you lose your personal allowance.

Solution: fully encash the bond before the tax year had been completed. There is no excess withdrawal as the calculation of gains on full surrenders includes withdrawals in the final policy year.

Assume an investment bond with a gain of £200,000 is surrendered and the client has other income of £70,000. If the bond was fully encashed in the previous tax year, it is assessed for tax in that current tax year. There would have been no impact on the personal allowance and the gain is taxed at 40% in 2009/10 (reduced by 20% if a gain in a UK bond). If encashed in this tax year, 2010/11, the personal allowance would be lost and some of the gain would be taxed at 50%. There would be top slicing relief and with no tax payable at the additional rate of 50% (and reduced by 20% as tax treated as paid in the bond.)

Timing when dealing with bonds is most important. The debate on whether to use a bond or collective investments continues. A bond merely defers income tax, which may or may not be payable. However, it does have uses for those seeking to minimise IHT (a discounted gift trust bond), and segments can be assigned to lower rated taxpayers who then mature those segments, and they pay the tax at a lower rate than the investor, possibly. There are strategies to avoid paying higher or additional rate tax on bonds, once the tax deferment period is over, or if you wish to pass income to a child or spouse. You may assign a bond segment to a third party, such as a child at school or university, who then surrenders it. The child will have a personal allowance for income tax purposes and will pay less tax.

Those who will be tax resident offshore when the bond matures can also escape a maturity liability, or reduce tax on maturity or encashment for the amount of time they lived outside the UK, even if they came back later. However, tax efficiency may favour the use of unit trusts and OEICS over that of a bond. One must also compare offshore with onshore bonds, as well as collective investments, when making comparisons.

Deposit accounts with deferred interest

Some bank accounts allow you to defer interest. The interest is only paid at the end or maturity of the investment, and tax is payable in that tax year.

Pension fund income deferral

If you have invested contributions into a personal pension fund, and are over age 55, you are eligible to take your tax-free cash. However, you may wish to do so but not wish to begin drawing a pension or annuity, or income at this time. You can defer the taking of income to a later date under drawdown by electing for nil income; or you can elect an annuity that is deferred. Deferring taxable income to a later date therefore saves immediate tax.

Discounted Gift Trust Bond (DGT)

Whilst the taking of income is a mandatory feature of the DGT, the income can be deferred through election at the outset.

State pension

You may defer the taking of your state pension. You can receive extra state pension if you defer for at least 5 weeks, or if deferral is for 12 months or more, you can choose to receive a lump sum. In actual fact, receiving a state pension is not automatic – you have to elect when it begins – if you do not so, it is automatically deferred.

Extra pension

By deferring your State Pension, your income is increased at a rate of 1% for every 5 weeks you put off drawing it. This equates to 10.4% extra a year.

For example, if your State Pension was £105 a week and you decided to delay drawing it for 5 years, the pension you would then receive would be £159.60 a week.

Lump sum

You also have the choice of a lump sum, as long as you delay drawing your pension for 12 consecutive months. The lump sum will equal the amount of pension you would have received plus interest. The rate of interest used equates to 2% above the Bank of England base rate.

The lump sum is taxable at the same rate as your other income.

You will not build up extra State Pension or a lump-sum payment while you are putting off claiming State Pension for the following reasons – usually if in receipt of benefits such as carer's allowance, short-term Incapacity benefit, another type of State Pension (apart from Graduated Retirement Benefit or shared additional pension), Severe Disablement Allowance, unemployability supplement, Widow's Pension, Widowed Mother's Allowance or any days you have been in prison because you were convicted of a criminal office. (See www.pensionsadvisoryservice.org.uk/state-pensions/deferring for further information.)

Capital Gains Tax deferral

Capital gains tax is payable at 18% for basic rate taxpayers and at 28% for higher rate taxpayers. Certain investments, such as qualifying EIS investments, enable you to defer an unlimited amount of capital gains. If this is the case, then you do not need to pay capital gains tax. You must reinvest the gain (not the tax on the gain) to obtain the deferral relief, and you have one year before the date of disposal leading to the capital gain and up to 3 years after the date of disposal to defer your gain. If you have already paid the capital gains tax, you can make the deferral investment and get back the tax paid (as long as within the criteria). At any time you can bring back the gain by selling the investment, for example, or so much of it as is required, and use your capital gains tax allowances for the tax year – in 2010/11 it is £10,100 per person. CGT is an optional tax. It need never be paid, as it can be deferred until death and then it dies with you. You can even set up your own company and use it for a qualifying trade and defer capital gains through it. Trusts may also defer capital gains in this way.

There are other reliefs associated with capital gains tax deferral, and these include CGT holdover reliefs – here an asset may be held with CGT holdover relief, and the gain is only crystallised when the asset is sold or disposed of. The gains are held over if the asset passes from one family member to another, or from a trust to a beneficiary – and tax must be paid when the asset is sold. These reliefs can defer tax and are very valuable.

You can defer the tax itself, or defer the income or capital gains that produce the taxable income or gain. Deferment now when you are a higher rate taxpayer to a later date when possibly a basic rate taxpayer, makes good tax and investment sense.

9

Reducing Your Tax Bill to Nil

There are legitimate ways to reduce your tax bill. All require expenditure, usually by investing. Assume Roger has sufficient investment monies and a higher risk profile. He is age under 65, and married. He has an IHT liability. The tax year is 2010/11. He usually makes up to £25,000 a year in pension contributions, and has an inheritance to invest. He does not like paying tax and this year decides to reduce his tax bill to nil.

Taxable Income	£149,999
Loses the personal allowance	0
(as income is over £100,000)	
Taxable	£149,999
Tax Payable	
At 20% on £37,400:	£7,480
At 40%: on £112,599:	£45,039

	£52,519
Less Pension contribution £24,650 at 20%	£4,930
Less VCT contribution £108,630 x 30%	£32,589
Less EIS contribution £75,000 x 20%	£15,000

Total deductions	£52,519

Tax Bill	**£0**

Cost: £183,630 invested into VCTs and EIS and £24,650 pension investment: £208,280

Net cost: £155,761 (after deducting the tax saved).

Roger could further reduce the net cost by taking 25% tax-free cash (of his contribution plus the HMRC uplift of 20%).

The EIS contribution could be backdated to the previous tax year for tax relief then. It also reduces IHT liability by £30,000 IHT after 2 years because of the EIS investment (£75,000 x 40%).

If EZ investments are used (this is the last tax year for an EZ investment), these reduce taxable income, not tax directly. This strategy could be more risky, if using limited recourse loans to fund the investment –

however, if there is a shortfall in available investment cash, this could be a useful strategy:

Taxable Income	£149,999	
Less EZ investment say [145,048]	£143,524	[qualifying expenditure]

Balance	£6,475	
Personal allowance*	£6,475	

Taxable income	£0	
Tax to pay	£0	

(*this is not lost as taxable income is reduced to below the £100,000 threshold)

Cost if using limited recourse loan:	
Investor cost:	£62,806
Loan:	£82,242

Total:	£143,048
Tax payable before investment:	£52,519

Investor net cost: £12,876 + loan interest + deferred loan payment [loan interest and repayment targeted from investment] Plus investment of £145,048.

Note I have not used the pension contribution in this example. If so, the EZ investment would be less to take into account the pension contribution tax relief – which would not apply if taxable income was reduced to nil.

Financial planning strategies

As you have seen with the above computations, tax can be significantly reduced, but cash outlay is required. Whilst investments should not be dictated by tax concerns, there are investors with higher risk profiles, who do wish to reduce tax.

We could have decided on a growth investment providing capital gains for the investor using the £10,100 personal exemption for part of our planning. However, for immediate tax relief purposes, tax reducing investments may be required.

Other factors to consider include safety and security of the investments made, and potential loss of capital (weighed against definite loss from the 'tax take' by HMRC). Other considerations may be capital gains tax deferral, reclaiming tax paid in the previous tax year, and IHT mitigation.

Overall, use the concepts of asset allocation for investment purposes, and client risk profiling, first, before offering higher risk investments (even if tax-reducing).

10

Investing for Children

I receive many queries each year on what type of investments parents can make for their children, or grandparents for their grandchildren, and the investments given below cover most of these aspects. Many are tax-efficient. Others are taxable, but the child has personal allowances, just like any adult has. These are a personal allowance for income tax purposes of £6,475 in the 2010/11 tax year (increasing to £7,475 in 2011/12), where the first £6,745 of taxable income is tax-free; and the capital gains tax personal allowance of £10,100. Children will have savings from many sources, including birthdays and pocket money. How they invest can be assisted by the selection below.

The investments considered are:

- Child's trust funds (CTF's)
- Friendly Society Policies
- Endowments and MIPs
- Trust bank accounts for children
- Designated account
- Bank and building society accounts
- National Savings Children's bonds
- Unit Trusts
- Investment Trusts
- Stakeholder pensions
- Cash and shares ISA – new Junior ISA
- The investment process – begin early
- Taxation of children's investments

Child's Trust Funds

From April 2005, all children born after September 1st 2002 will have received a voucher from the Government to the value of £250 (from January 2005). If the child is born into a family where the household income is £16,190 or less, then the initial payment is £500.

Since April 2010, a child eligible for Disability Living Allowance also gets a yearly top-up of £100, or £200 if the child has a severe disability.

Now the axe will fall on these payments.

From 1 August, payments at birth will be reduced from £250 to £50 for better off families, and £500 to £100 for lower income families [household income of less than £16,190]; and payments at age seven stopped.

All payments will be stopped from 1 January 2011.

This money was to be invested into a Child's Trust Fund, which will have tax-free returns. Parents and grandparents, friends and family can add another £1,200 a year. The fund can be encashed from age 18. There is a wide range of investment options to choose from. These include stakeholder style products as well as cash-based schemes. For maximum growth potential, one would want exposure to equities.

Assuming an investment return of 6%, if the £250 was invested, with a further £1,200 a year to age 18, the value of the fund would be £39,577, enough to pay for 3 years at University.

Because the Government does not have the budget for CTFs, they are to be scrapped from 1st January 2011. Existing CTFs will be allowed to continue until maturity. The tax-free element will continue. No tax is paid on any income or gains in the account. Importantly, the current rules regarding parental gifts to children will not apply. The parent will therefore not be taxed on any income arising over £100.

Family and friends will still be able to add up to £1,200 a year into the account.

The government will not withdraw the money it has already put in the account. It has been said (by David White of the Children's Mutual) that The Child Trust Fund is the single most successful savings policy to date and this sort of short-term cut does not address the pressing need for families to save, or recognise the significant benefit to society that the Child Trust Fund will bring from 2020 as maturing funds return an anticipated £2.96bn each year to the economy.

It was recently announced that a Junior ISA will become available for young savers, but will not be funded by the Government.

Friendly Society policies

A Friendly Society policy is similar to an endowment policy, and in fact most use with profits funds. Restricted in the amount you can invest, the returns are tax-free if the investment runs for at least 10 years. The minimum investments are as low as £10 per month or £100 per annum, the maximum £25 per month or £270 per annum. Each child and parent per family can take out an investment of this type. Most invest into with-profits funds, however, Friendly Societies have special tax treatment and often their returns are better than conventional life offices. There is no minimum age, but the maximum is age 80. The investment fund is exempt from CGT, corporation and income taxes.

Parents can pay for their children's investments, as can grandparents for grandchildren. Returns are tax-free after ten years. Particularly popular is a Friendly Society 'Baby Bond', which gives exposure to equity investments and provides for tax-free growth and payouts. The maximum entry age for a baby bond is age 16, and most give limited life cover if the child is over ten years old.

Endowment and MIP plans

These are regular savings plans with monthly premiums. These plans are set up to run for a minimum period of ten years. They are not as tax-efficient as Friendly Society Plans, but do pay out a tax-free amount. They can be kept going after maturity and income can be drawn from them, if required. They may suit those who have utilised their Friendly Society premium limits. Charging structures can be high, and have been high in the past, but are now coming down. However, these plans do include life cover, which is a requirement for some.

Maximum investment plans (MIPs)

Largely out of favour at present, but there are a few companies around with above-average returns. The monthly investment is into a life assurance policy for a minimum period of 10 years (although the proceeds can be withdrawn after seven and a half years, tax-free).

The returns are tax-free, but the life office will have suffered tax on its internal funds. All include life cover, with a payout on death. MIPs are unit-linked life assurance policies, with a large percentage of the premiums invested. The minimum age is age 12 and the maximum age is 80. You can take a tax-free income after ten years, so long as you continue to pay at least 50% of the original premium.

The minimum premium is from £20 per month, depending on the provider. If death occurs within the ten-year policy term, the greater of the guaranteed death benefit or the unitised investment fund will be paid.

The MIP provides a tax-free capital sum and tax-free income after ten years; the capital can be left to grow after ten years; and you can continue to pay premiums for a further ten years. Policies can be underwritten on a joint life basis, payable on first or second death. A series of MIPs can be taken out to mature at different dates when they will be required. This may suit for school and university fees planning. Some may have loan facilities, should cash be needed earlier.

Endowment assurance policies

You must be aged between 12 to 75 years to effect an endowment assurance policy.

For those wishing to build up a tax-free lump sum over a long term, these policies offer a relatively low-risk investment medium to do so. The policy is for a minimum period of ten years for tax-free proceeds (although after seven and a half years proceeds can be withdrawn tax-free on a ten-year plan). Policies are either with profits or unit-linked, and a wide range of investment funds are usually offered.

Unlike Friendly Society policies, corporation tax and CGT will be charged on the income or capital gains arising on the life company's funds. You may also have to be medically examined, and life cover may be expensive. The charging structure could also be high, although providers are reducing charges to make their products more saleable. One must distinguish between endowments that are pure savings oriented with a minimum of life cover, as opposed to, say, one required for a mortgage, where the life cover requirement is higher. Early surrender could result in penalties and loss of investment capital, so view this a longer-term investment.

You can also purchase a second-hand with-profits endowment policy and pay the premiums on it until maturity. The payout for qualifying policies is free of income tax, but may be subject to capital gains tax, although you have an exemption of £10,100 per person in 2010/11.

Endowment policies have largely fallen out of favour over recent years, as a result of over-estimating returns, and have been seen as poor value. However, Friendly Society policies are popular and MIPs may see a resurgence.

Trust accounts for children

Bare trusts

When you want the money you give the child to become their property, open a bare trust. You hold the investments in trust in your name on behalf of the child. At age 18, the child gains full control of the investments. For tax purposes, the investments are treated as those of the child.

A savings provider can provide you with a 'declaration of trust' form, where you intend to gift the investment to the child. The declaration is sent to the local Inland Revenue office to be stamped and returned to you.

Any investment made by you in this way falls out of your estate for inheritance tax purposes (and could also be part of your annual £3,000 IHT-free gift allowance, or from surplus payments out of normal expenditure).

You can open a bank or building society account for your child. The account may be opened in your name, but with the child as the beneficiary. Complete the BR85 Inland Revenue form, given to you by the bank or building society, so that interest earned can be paid gross. Income of more than £100 in a tax year will be taxed in your hands (£200 if two parents), where the parent has made the gift in the first place. Saving the child benefit (if you still get it after the budget cuts)in this way is a gift from the parent to the child.

Once sufficient funds have accumulated, you may wish to invest these into an investment fund. You buy the investment in your name, adding the child's name or initials to designate the holding as being held on the child's behalf. The parents would be the trustees of the bare trust, and registered owners of the shares or investment, but the child is the beneficial owner. The HMRC does not need to be informed that a bare trust has been set up, but keep all records and documentation in case there is an enquiry.

Designated account

A designated account keeps you in control of any money gifted to a child. When you set up a savings or investment plan, you hold it in your own name, but 'designate' it in the child's name. You will be liable for any tax that may be payable. The investment or savings account remains as part of your assets; you decide when to give the money to your child.

Bank and building society accounts

There is a wide range of children's savings accounts available – some generous with their interest, others poor. Many providers offer incentives to child savers, so shop around. Children's deposit accounts must be in the parent's name if the child is under age seven, but designated with the child's initials. If the child makes the deposit (or a third party other than a parent), the child will be taxed (no tax payable if within the personal allowance of £6,475 in 2010/11); if a parent makes it and interest is over £100 (one parent, £200 if both), the parent is taxed on the interest. Obtain HMRC form BR85 to ensure interest is paid gross and tax-free. At www.moneymadeclear.org.uk are calculators for savings rates, including the best savers rates for children's investments. For example, currently Clydesdale Bank has a 5 year children's savings bond paying 4.25% annually – the minimum is £50. The maximum age is age 16 for this bank account. Yorkshire Bank offers the same type of account.

National Savings Children's Bonds

A National Savings Children's Bond is available to children under the age of 16, but can be held until the child turns 21. These are 5- year bonds that pay a fixed rate of interest, tax-free. A bonus is paid at the end of the 5th year. The minimum investment is £25 and the maximum £3,000. After five years, the bond can run for another five years, but at a new interest rate. The investment can be held in the name of child or parent.

If the bond is kept for the full five year period, a bonus is payable.

The child takes control of the bond at age 16 and can re-invest it into another bond, also tax-free, until they reach age 21.

Children's Bonus Bonds Issue 34, has a guaranteed compound rate over 5 years including 5th anniversary bonus, and tax-free, paying 2.5% AER – *this is available.*

You can invest tax-free for your child's future in their own name. All returns on Children's Bonus Bonds are completely tax-free for both child and parent. "Tax-free" means you don't have to pay any UK Income Tax or Capital Gains Tax. This can be cashed in early, but no interest is earned if cash in within the first year.

Unit trusts

The investor (no minimum age) purchases units in a trust, the price of which is determined by the value of the underlying securities in which the trust invests. The investment should be for at least 5 years – over the longer term, an equity investment should produce better returns than cash and bonds – say 10 years. Dividends should be re-invested into the unit trust funds.

The unit trust is registered in the name of the parent for the child in a designated account, until the child reaches age 18, when the fund becomes theirs. The child will have an annual capital gains tax allowance (in 2010/11 this is £10.100) for any investment gains arising in the unit trust, making gains tax-free up to that amount.

Investment trusts

There is no minimum age limit, but if under age 18, the investment trust is registered in the name of the parent as above for unit trusts. An investment trust gives access to stock market investments and there are a number of investment trust child savings plans available. Some can be designated as a bare trust. Most start at £25 per month, or a minimum lump sum of £250. Reduced charges apply for many children's investments, so shop around.

Stakeholder pensions

These are absolutely no good if investing on behalf of a youngster if planning to use it to pay education fees – as the minimum age to take a pension is age 55. However, there are no age limits on entering into a stakeholder pension plan. A baby can have one and benefit from a 20% tax uplift from the government paid in to the pension plan – even if you are not a taxpayer. The maximum you can invest each year without earnings is £3,600 (of which you pay £2,880 and the government pays £720). This is a method of real long- term savings that could give your child a significant pension at retirement. Contributions can be monthly or by lump sum.

Cash ISA and the new Junior ISA

If you like, you can open both a cash ISA and a stocks and shares ISA in the same tax year. However, the total amount you put in cannot exceed £10,200.

So you could invest £5,100 into each, or you could invest £2,000 in a cash ISA and £8,200 in a stocks and shares ISA. You can't however have £6,000 in a cash ISA and £4,200 in the stocks and shares version, as the cash limit is just £5,100.

You can have both types of ISAs with the same provider, or you can have them with two separate companies. Most ISA providers will also let you combine cash ISAs from previous years into one big cash ISA. The same applies to stocks and shares ISAs.

One of the new rules added in recent years is that you can decide to convert a cash ISA into a stocks and shares ISA. This allows you to invest in a wider variety of products that should provide a greater return over the long term. But you *can't* do the reverse, and convert a stocks and shares ISA into a cash one.

You can invest £5,100 into a cash ISA, obtaining the best rates from banks and building societies. A 16-year old can invest into a cash ISA. For regular savings, you can invest into a one-year ISA bond say with better interest rates. For ISA investments generally, you must be age 18. The Government has recently announced a new Junior ISA for children, which will grow tax-free and have tax-free gains and income. No details are currently available, but the Junior ISA is set to replace the CTF. The Government will not be contributing to it.

Investing on your child's behalf

Begin as early as possible. Long term investment returns in the UK Stock market have been about 11% p.a. since 1918 ('Motley Fool- why investing makes sense'). Probably a bit less now after the past few years of stock market falls, but rising markets could be coming back.

The table shows what investing £100 at various growth rates are over various terms:

Year	4%	8%	12%
1	£100	£100	£100
5	£122	£147	£176
10	£148	£216	£311
18	£203	£400	£769
21	£228	£503	£1,080

The stock market is not without its risk, but these risks are smoothed over time for performance, and one must be 'in the market' to benefit from it. 0-2 % is what a savings account may pay right now, 8% could be a return from a tracker fund, and 12% is for lucky stock pickers. The capital in bank and building society accounts does not grow (although you will earn interest on your money), but exposure to the stock markets will have a chance of growth. Sure, there will be fluctuations as markets rise and fall, but generally, growth is expected over the investment term. Some building societies have investment bonds that guarantee your capital and give you interest and investment growth – for the more conservative investor. However, most investors are wary of bank or other guarantees.

Taxation on children's investments

Each child has an individual personal allowance for income tax of £6,475 in the 2010/11 tax year. Otherwise taxable income received within that band is tax-free. There is also a capital gains tax exemption for every person (no matter what your age), of £10,100 in 2010/11.

How income arising, or capital gains arising will be taxed, depends on the source of funds to the child. If the source is from parents, the general rule is they are taxed on any interest over £100 in any one year (£200 if gifts are made separately by both parents) – except for interest arising on the National Savings Children's Bonus Bond and CTF investments. Under £100 a year, it is treated as the child's income.

Once the child reaches age 18, the income is treated as his or her own.

If the money came from anyone else – grandparents, relatives – then any income arising is treated as the child's own for tax purposes.

Always complete HMRC form BR85 for bank and building society accounts to have income paid gross and not subject to tax deductions. This will hold for your child until age 16, when the child registers personally. Any tax previously deducted from the child's interest can be reclaimed up to 6 years.

If the child receives dividends from shares, unit trusts and investment trusts, this is paid net of a tax credit, currently 10%. Basic rate taxpayers have no further tax to pay, higher rate taxpayers will pay further tax, and non-taxpayers cannot reclaim the tax credit.

For capital gains arising, the child has a personal exempt amount (£10,100 in 2010/11) that can be used – it does not matter what the source of the capital is. It may be better to invest into capital growth investments and utilise the annual exemption to withdraw capital gains arising within the exemption.

To sum up, you may invest for your child, or third parties can do so. The sooner the process begins, the better the long-term results. There are many investment options available, depending on your risk profile, age, and stage of the investment process.

11

Investing for the Elderly

Just about everyone in the UK on reaching age 50 receives a welcome pack from Saga – it must cost them a fortune! However, they are fully aware that the 50+ market has more investment money than age groups below that. As you get older and children have flown the nest, and you then retire at age 65, you will have lump sums to invest. Most investors will be cautious, with a set limit of funds available to invest. Many will require income to supplement their retirement income. Others will require planning for care home fees, and advice on aspects such as equity release and how to invest their money.

Tax planning

There are increased personal allowances for the 65 year olds to 74 and again for those aged 75 and over.

Under age 65:	£6,475
Age 65- 74:	£9,490
Age 75+	£9,640

The first £9,640 is free of income tax. However, beware the age allowance trap. If you have taxable income above £22,900 and are age 65+, then your personal allowance reduces on a £1 for £2 basis until it reaches the basic personal allowance of £6,475 in 2010/11. So if you have pension income of say £22,000 per annum, anything taxable over £22,900 will lose your personal allowances. This is akin to an additional tax on your earnings. In this example, you could only earn a further £900 before falling into the age allowance trap. Your married couples allowance is also reduced. Then if you earn over £100,000, you lose your personal allowance on a similar basis, making increasing taxable income more expensive for you.

You also have a capital gains tax allowance of £10,100 in the 2010/11 tax year. This means that you can take an otherwise taxable gain as tax-free 'income' by cashing in investments to provide it. Bearing in mind the age allowance trap, you should consider taking growth from investments and not taxable income as part of your financial and investment planning.

There are other traps to be wary of. If receiving means tested benefits, additional income or capital could reduce these or you could lose these altogether. Having investments and income that count towards means testing could ensure that care fees are paid by you, and not the local council or authority, who would otherwise contribute.

Income strategy

It is therefore important to align your investment strategy accordingly with your tax strategy. For example, 5% tax deferred withdrawals from an investment bond, does not count as income for the age allowance trap, nor would income from ISAs as this is tax-free.

I have shown current savers rates in previous chapters. However, many elderly investors are very investment risk averse and would only consider bank and building society deposits, or national savings and investments. The current best 5 year term deposit rate is 4.55% paying interest annually. After tax that interest amount will be reduced. Inflation will drive down its real value even further. However, some investments are or were available because of your more advanced years. The NS & I offered pensioners' guaranteed income or capital bonds, but no longer do so. Some banks and building societies may offer a higher rate to you if age over 55 (or higher) – always enquire for their best terms.

Otherwise, the general investment scenario applies equally to the elderly as it does to those far younger.

Annuities

The one area where age could be on your side is with annuities.

If going into (or already in a care home), an immediate needs annuity is assessed on you medically and provides a guaranteed stream of income for life. If paid directly to the care fees home, this is free of income tax. A recent client aged 88 receives annuity income of over 19% of her investment per annum – and this escalates each year at 8% to take care of fees' inflation. These annuities can be capital protected.

The older you are, the higher the annuity rate. Even though generally annuity rates are at their lowest for the past 40 years, for some personal annuities (not from pension funds, but where you use your own capital), reasonable annual rates can be achieved to provide a regular stream of income, which is tax-efficient (only the interest portion is taxable).

Pensions as investments

The other investment possibility for those aged between 55 and 75 is to make single premium pension contribution investments (even if you have no relevant earnings, you can have £3,600 contributed to a personal pension plan each year. Of this you pay £2,880 and the HMRC pays in £720 to make up the £3,600 contribution. You therefore have a return of at least 20% on your money every time you make this investment. You can then take 25% in tax-free cash (based on your investment and the HMRC's investment), and the balance of the fund buys you an income for life, which is taxable. If you are a higher rated taxpayer, in addition, the HMRC will give you back another 20% in tax relief (or 30% if an additional rated taxpayer). This is probably the most tax-efficient investment you can make.

Inheritance tax-deductible investments

You may be asset rich and have an inheritance tax problem. You require a regular stream of income, but would also like to have some of your investment out of your estate for inheritance tax purposes. If under age 89 (the HMRC is reluctant to give this discount anyone older), you can be medically assessed for a discounted gift trust investment. This is an investment bond that is in trust and provides a stream of income that is tax deferred. The investment cannot be cashed in at any time. However, it immediately reduces your estate for inheritance tax purposes by a proportion and if you survive for 7 years, by the balance of the investment leaving your estate for inheritance tax purposes. The balance of the investment is for the benefit of your heirs. All growth in the investment is out of your estate for inheritance tax purposes. Variations on this kind of investment include a gift and loan trust investment, where you receive non taxable loan payments that are returned by the investment in later years.

Inheritance tax allowances include making gifts out of income (unlimited, so long as this does not reduce your standard of living), potential exempt transfers – gifts that are out of your estate if you survive for 7 years; the nil rate band of £325,000 for inheritance taxable assets, to name a few.

Investments such as EIS are out of your estate after 2 years.

Proper planning is essential to align your income requirements with capital growth and also tax strategies.

12

Trust Investments

The investment landscape is changing. On the one hand, the Government has brought in new penal taxation from 6.4.2010 on income arising from investments, such as interest, and other income, such as rents. The new tax on income will be 50% (rising from 40% – a 25% increase) and that on dividends will be 42.5% (rising from 32.5% – a 30.76% increase). At least for individuals, the new tax level of 50% from 2010/2011 will apply for taxable income over £150,000 (with a loss of personal allowances for taxable incomes over £100,000 on a £1 for every £2 basis). For trusts, there is no such 'luxury', and after the £1,000 basic rate level for trusts, discretionary trust income is taxed at 50% from 2010/2011. The effect of the present and increased trust taxation rates will be to reduce cash flows and income payments for beneficiaries.

For current and new investments this will have to be borne in mind, as it severely affects cash-flowing.

The previous and current trust tax position

	2009/10	2010/2011
Tax on income and interest	40%	50%
Tax on dividends	32.5%	42.5%
Standard trust rate on first £1,000	20%	20%
Capital Gains Tax	18%	28%
Trust exemption Capital Gains Tax (apportioned to up to 5 trusts)	£5,050	£5,050
Inheritance Tax rate	40%	40%
Lifetime rate for CLTs over nil rate band	20%	20%
Nil rate band	£325,000	£325,000

Individual personal allowances (if a beneficiary is taxable)

	2010/11	
To age 65	£6,475	*Progressively lose*
65-74	£9,490	*these allowances*
75 +	£9,640	*on income over*
Age allowance income limit	£22,900	*£100,000*
CGT allowance	£10,100	

Individual income tax rates

Starting savings rate   10%

On income up to £2,440 but only applies to savings income. If taxable non-savings income is above this Limited, the starting rate does not apply

Basic rate	20%
On taxable income up to	£37,400
Higher rate	40%
On taxable income over	£150,000
Additional rate	50%
Dividend income – lower rate	10%
Dividend income – higher rate	32.5%
Additional rate	42.5%

The challenge for income remains great, as we currently have a 0.5% base rate, with very low interest rates on investments. Often the better interest rates are simply not available to trustees, although they may be available to individuals. If invested in bank deposits with a return of say 2% gross p.a., after trust taxation at 50%, the outlook for returns on investment from conventional investments looks bleak. If dividends, trust taxation at 42.5% in 2010/2011 will severely affect dividend income.

The following are the 'Drivers' that will change the way trustees think about cash-flowing and what investments to have.

Trust efficiency drivers (investments and tax)

1. A shift to investments that defer tax on income, or tax-free or partially taxable investments.

2. A partial shift from income or interest-bearing investments to dividend-bearing investments as the overall tax rate is lower.

3. Greater use of investment bonds that allow tax deferred withdrawals at up to 5% p.a. of the original capital invested. These withdrawals are seen as capital in nature when withdrawn at up to 5%, but are income taxable at maturity (with top-slicing reliefs applying). Trusts must therefore be able to appoint capital to beneficiaries.

4. A shift to taking growth (as 'income') by way of capital gains from investments, where the tax on capital gains is 28%. The problem may be that to achieve growth returns (which have not been generally evident over the past two years, but are improving), may require a higher risk rating for trustees, and cannot be relied upon for regular income.

5. A shift to more general individual tax planning for maximum effect. The use of a beneficiary's tax allowances and the ability to reclaim tax paid

by trustees is paramount here. For example, where a grandparent sets up an A & M trust for grandchild beneficiaries, and income flows from the trust to those beneficiaries, then the individual beneficiary personal allowances can be used (with tax paid by trustees reclaimed). This scenario would not work where the settler is a parent, or self-interested, as trust income would then be taxed in the parent's hands and not the beneficiary's.

6. Greater individual beneficiary tax planning may be required, where for example the beneficiary is a non-resident Commonwealth citizen as from 2010/11 onwards, the entitlement to UK personal allowances and reliefs will be withdrawn for non-residents, who would otherwise qualify for them solely by virtue of their being Commonwealth citizens (although double taxation treaties may apply).

7. To lessen the impact of 10 year periodic and trust termination charges, and capital appointments (capital leaving the trust), possibly for more income and capital gains to leave the trust to the benefit of individuals (who can offset tax) as a strategy during the trust term, rather than intermittently or at the trust end.

8. A change in trustee risk profiling and asset allocation to accommodate investments that work efficiently, but may be higher risk (trading investment risk for increased efficiency, as the incidence of high taxation reduces the investment return in any event by up to 50% from 2010/2011).

9. Overall the need to take into account the Policy Statement and Guidelines (PSG) provisions under the Trustee Act 2000. Gone are the days when trustees can rely on a half to one-page policy statement and guidelines that are very general. Detailed examination of all aspects will be a core part of the PSG in the future, including tax planning at the point of sale and ongoing tax planning with regard to investments used, tax arising, tax mitigation, liquidity of trusts, and future cash-flowing. Our PSG's are currently around 40 pages in length, and will increase in the future to take into account the effect of taxation at all levels. The anomaly in the **Trustee Act 2000** where the duty to consult beneficiaries not being delegable (to a financial planner, for example) where only trustees can consult and give effect to the wishes of the beneficiaries (**section 13(4)** of **TA 2000**) is an anachronism. Not all trustees are fully conversant with tax law and provisions, and for a full PSG to be effected properly, the beneficiaries' tax position and allowances available etc., needs to be an integral part of financial planning. Trustees who do not attend to all aspects of diversification under the standard investment criteria under **section 4(1)** leave themselves open to attack – ' *a trustee must have regard to the suitability of the trust of the investment, and, where appropriate, the need for diversification of the trust's investments'.* The core criteria are set out in **section 4(3)** of **TA 2000**.

10. An important need to urgently review all existing trusts. There is a statutory duty of care applying now and under **section 1** and **section 2** (and **schedule 1**) of the Act defines when the duty will apply. **Section 4(2)** requires the trustees to keep investments of the trust under review, and to consider, whether, in the light of standard investment criteria, they should be varied. This provision codifies the common law position, under which 'a trustee with a power of investment must undertake periodic reviews of the investments held by the trust' *(Nestle v National Westminster Bank plc (no 2) [1993] 1 WLR 1260, 1282G, per Leggatt L.J.).*

11. Trustees must be motivated to comply fully with the **Trustee Act 2000**, and at the very least, ensure that all trusts (the Act applies to all trusts, whenever established) are regularly reviewed. Many trustees have not realigned or balanced investments or applied ongoing suitability criteria or diversification criteria since the inception of their trusts. Beneficiaries will look to the Trustees where trust compliance has not been attended to, and they feel they have suffered loss. Imagine tax losses (costs) of up to 50%, where there has been no tax planning and no future scenario planning and cash-flowing.

Role of the financial planner

The financial planner (investment manager, bank manager etc.) is known as the nominated adviser under the **Trustee Act 2000**. The financial planner can only take instructions *after* his terms of business and client agreement has been signed, and then only on the receipt of the Policy Statement and Guidelines (PSG) from the Trustees as prescribed by the **Trustee Act 2000**. If the PSG is poorly constructed or is non-existent, you can count on the advice flowing from it to be poor. This is a highly specialised area, and very few financial planners are capable of undertaking it. Yet the investments in all UK trusts is said to exceed £20 billion in value, and this is an excellent area for professional trustees to be working hand in hand with qualified financial planners. By not providing the financial planner with a properly constructed PSG, the trustees are doing the financial planner a disservice. Note that **section 5** of **TA 2000** states that the trustee, when considering the exercise of a power of investment or carrying out a review of the investments of the trust, *must obtain and consider proper advice* about how, in view of the standard investment criteria the power to invest should be exercised or the investments of the trust be varied (**sections 5(1) and 5(2)**). 'Proper advice' is defined in **section 5(4)** where other expert skills may also be relevant. More importantly, **section 15** relates to the delegation of asset management functions by trustees. That includes the investment of trust assets and the acquisition, disposal and management of trust property (**section 15(5)**).

The terms of an agreement authorising the agent to exercise asset management functions on behalf of the trustees must be in writing or evidenced in writing (**section 15(1)**) and must require the agent to secure compliance with the trustees' guidance as to how the functions are to be exercised for the time being (**section 15(2)**).

This Guidance must be in writing or evidenced in writing (**section 15(4)**) and must be framed with a view to ensuring the functions will be exercised in the best interests of the trust (**section 15 (3)**).

The financial planner derives his financial planning instructions (and delegable powers) from the PSG. His or her role is to construct the trust financial plan, taking into account standard investment criteria, which includes tax planning and diversification issues, if required. The objectives of the trust are taken into account, including those of beneficiaries – life tenants and remaindermen for income and capital, and also the objectives of the trustees, which may include tax efficiency and other aspects. The **Trustee Act 2000** provides for ongoing reviews and reports, and sanctions of the financial planner, investment managers etc. who do not comply. It is therefore equally important for the financial planner to be protected, as it is for the trustees, in the giving of advice and in reporting.

The financial planner, taking all circumstances into account, then recommends an investment strategy to meet with the objectives of the trustees and the need for income and capital growth and investment disposals over the term of the trust (or as decided). Asset allocation and risk profiling of the trustees is taken into account, and investments are recommended and implemented accordingly. Monitoring and review periods are usually every 6 months.

Payment of tax – discretionary trusts

This is a complicated area and depends on how the trust was set up, and what sort of trust it is. The trustees are liable for tax on income at the tax rate of 50% in the tax year 2010/2011, and dividends at 42.5% in 2010/11. In certain circumstances, the beneficiary's tax rates can be used, and tax reclaimed from the trustees. Certainly income and dividends accumulated in a trust will be taxed at the trust rate first, before being paid to beneficiaries. Capital gains are taxed at 28%.

Where income is paid to a beneficiary, tax could be paid by a settlor if a settlor – interested trust. It could be taxed on the beneficiary if there is no connection to the settlor, for example, where a grandparent sets up an A & M trust for a grandchild to benefit, the income is taxed in the beneficiary's hands, and tax paid by the trustees can be reclaimed.

An area that requires attention is in relation to what expenses are deducted by the trustees and from where. For example, expenses may be deducted from capital and not taxable income, depending on how they are categorised. This could have the effect of reducing income for an income beneficiary, or capital for the trust (and subsequently the remaindermen.)

Investment strategy and tax strategy

Investment strategy must be aligned with overall tax strategy to create cash flow efficiency.

We are currently in an investment cycle of very low growth returns (although improving over the past few months) and much reduced income returns from most investments. Taxation will reduce cash flows by 42.5% to 50% in this tax year. The investment process must be managed properly at all times, not only from inception, and regular reviews should flag up issues that need addressing. It is therefore most important that the structure of investments is properly planned to avoid long-term cash flows and cash reduction.

Importance of cash and liquidity

What is cash required for, as liquidity for trusts is of prime importance?

1. Trust income commitments for beneficiaries and life tenants – be they single payments or regular payments.
2. Appointing capital to beneficiaries where required to do so
3. Making investments
4. Purchases such as fixed property
5. Trust running costs and disbursements
6. Tax to pay; stamp duties etc.
7. Fees to advisers

Trust liquidity is crucial for all trusts. Money will be required at different periods for any of the reasons above. For example, general disbursements require continuous cash flow ability, as do income payments. One does not wish to encash assets to provide for cash flow as there may be tax implications on encashment, or assets may be difficult to cash in due to market conditions. This could cause the trust and its beneficiaries' untold problems, especially if income is expected and relied upon.

The importance of how to structure investments for the most optimum effect cannot be stressed enough. This also means defining the tax structure of the trust and its beneficiaries and how their personal allowances and tax rates can be best used. A prime example here is for an investment made that produces taxable income, but where it can be taxed in the beneficiary's hands ultimately. So a 66 year old has £9,490 in personal allowances before tax is paid at any rate. Obviously current taxable income must be taken into account, but any personal allowance than can be used in part will reduce the overall tax rate – the basic rate is at 20% whereas the trust rate is at 50%. It may even be a strategy for the trustees to decide to accumulate income in the beneficiary's hands, rather than the trust's hands for tax reasons – the increase in income could well be double.

The shift to investment bonds where income can be taken on a tax deferred basis, as opposed to other investments, becomes more important with increasing tax rates for trusts. Withdrawals may be paid to beneficiaries 'tax-free' during the term of the bond. On encashment or near maturity there are strategies to minimise the incidence of taxation, such as assigning segments of a bond to the beneficiary who may be a basic rate taxpayer – this is treated as tax paid and no further tax is paid.

However, if you require an investment with access to capital, then perhaps the bond route is not for you, and you may need unit trusts or OEICS or similar investments, where the growth can be encashed and capital gains tax paid at 28%, after the CGT exemption of £5,050 for trusts.

The above is merely a synopsis to cover appropriate investment and tax strategy.

Trusts and IHT

One of the biggest tax giveaways is Inheritance Tax (IHT), which we overpay to the tune of £1.9 billion a year. I describe IHT as 'a bill which arrives after you depart', because it is paid by your estate after your death. If you have assets (including your home) worth over £325,000, then IHT could take care of up two-fifths (40%) of your estate over this 'nil-rate band'

Therefore it is important to maximise use of the inheritance tax exemptions. For example, the annual exemption is £3,000 (and can be doubled the first time you use it). Thus, £12,000 annual exemptions are immediately available for a married couple. You can give away this amount without paying IHT on it. It can be used to pay premiums on a life policy held in trust, or to a trust investment requiring annual payments.

Write life policies into trust – including existing ones to save IHT. Many life policies are not in trust and therefore fall into your estate where inheritance tax may be applied to the proceeds. Imagine losing 40% of your life policy proceeds on death for want of a simple trust deed. In addition, if in trust, this bypasses probate and the funds are immediately available to your heirs.

Similarly with pension death benefits – direct these to a suitable trust to avoid IHT on subsequent death of member's surviving spouse/civil partner, whilst still enabling them to benefit.

Gift surplus income (that do not reduce a standard of living) to reduce an existing IHT liability – you can use income from drawdown and ASP for these purposes. Gifts can be made into trust and are unlimited.

Gifts can therefore be made to trust to reduce IHT liabilities. Create trusts on different dates and make gifts in the correct order. (see *Inheritance Tax Simplified* for all of these strategies). Other gifts that can be made to reduce your estate assets are as follows:

- Gifts of up to £250 per person (per annum)
- Gifts in consideration of marriage/civil partnership of £5,000 by a parent, £2,500 by a grandparent, or £1,000 by any other person.

- Gifts may even be made to charity or political parties and these will reduce your estate accordingly.

Document the unused nil rate band amounts for future use by a surviving spouse/civil partner. The nil rate band is currently £325,000 and it is frozen at this level to 2016. The unused portion of a nil rate band is transferable to a spouse or a civil partner.

Investments for trusts

As far as trust investments are concerned, the trustees can make any type of investment that an individual can legally make, except for highly personalised investments such as ISA's and VCTs. It can invest into bank and building society investments, structured settlements, property, gold bullion etc. However, some investments will be more beneficial for the trust than others, and certainly more tax-efficient. Because of the very high incidence of trust taxation, certainly for discretionary trusts, trustees will seek to take more capital growth as income and to make use of tax wrappers, such as investment bonds. Investment bonds enable capital to be drawn down and used as income without an immediate charge to tax. Tax is deferred to the time of a chargeable event, such as the surrender or maturity of the bond. Tax strategies will include assigning segments of the investment bond to lower rated taxpayer beneficiaries, who can then offset their own income tax personal allowances (as investment bonds are subject to income tax, not capital gains tax). If that 5% return was taxable in the trust then it would immediately reduce to 2.5%. You can double your income by investing trust investments through an investment bond. Some investment bonds held by trusts invest only in fixed interest securities, others invest into managed or discretionary managed portfolios – gains that would have been taxable in the trust if not in the investment bond tax wrapper – are now sheltered from tax. Note that if income is accumulated from investments like unit trusts, then tax is payable, even if it is not paid to the trust, but reinvested.

Individuals can make use of discounted gift trusts (DGTs) for immediate IHT relief. An assessment is undertaken based on your age, status and health and the HMRC allows part of the investment immediately to come out of your estate for inheritance tax purposes. The balance, if under the nil rate band falls out of your estate for IHT purposes, after you have survived for 7 years. If you die within the seven year period, then taper relief applies.

Although higher risk, some trusts may wish to defer a capital gain through making an EIS investment. CGT at 28% need not be paid until the gain is recrystallised. EIS investments to defer CGT should always be seen as higher risk. Most trustees will therefore pay the capital gains tax, rather than take on an investment that invests into unquoted companies. Whilst loss reliefs will apply, there will be no income tax relief for a trust making an EIS investment.

The great need for trusts to satisfy income beneficiaries (life tenants) will be a major challenge for trustees in the future, and how they set up their investments or modify them after reviews. Tax and investment planning go hand in hand, and include the beneficiaries and their tax status and tax returns and reporting – the ambit of trustees will become a lot wider in the future as they seek to minimise taxes and increase effectiveness.

13

Investing for Businesses

Businesses will include companies, partnerships, LLPs and sole traders. The investments and planning information given for individuals will apply to sole traders, partners and LLP members. The focus in this chapter is aimed at companies in the main.

Companies do not have personal tax allowances, and any capital gains are added to corporation taxable income. Companies can make investments that are tax-efficient, and like any business, the investments it makes must be wholly and necessarily for the benefit of the business to be tax deductible to the business. Businesses can invest into research and development and obtain 100% allowances, and into plant and machinery and obtain up to 100% allowances. For energy saving and environmentally beneficial equipment, low CO_2 emission cars, natural gas and hydrogen refuelling equipment, there is a first year allowance of 100%. There is an annual investment allowance of 100% on the first £100,000 of expenditure (excludes cars and expenditure already qualifying for the 100% first year allowance). If expenditure does not qualify for such allowances, they may qualify for the writing down allowances at 10% or 20% and even 1% on buildings. There is even an enterprise zone allowance at 100% for the conversion of parts of business premises into flats or business premises renovation.

A business can invest in its people by paying them salaries, or into pension funds for their retirement benefits. These are expenses deductible from profits for tax purposes. So businesses invest in themselves and obtain tax reliefs for doing so. If the business qualifies under the EIS rules, people can invest in the business and obtain personal tax reliefs at 20% of the investment made up to £500,000. Businesses can also make investments of their surplus profits or cash.

Corporation tax

With effect from March 2011, the main rate of corporation tax for companies with profits above the upper limit of £1.5 million will be reduced by 1% to 27%. Further reductions will be made in the following tax years to 26% in 2012-13, 25% in 2013-14 and 24% for 2014-15.

Also from next April 2012, the small profits rate of corporation tax for those companies with profits below the lower limit of £300,000 will be reduced from 21% to 20%.

Currently though the main levels of corporation tax are:

First £300,000	21%
Next £1,200,000	29.75%
Over £1,500,000	28%

Capital gains, after deductions and indexation are added to taxable profits. There is no CGT exemption, as there is with individuals or trusts.

Businesses may make investments in the same way as individuals. However, the same tax rates and reliefs that apply for individuals, do not apply to companies, but will apply for sole traders and partnership members.

The following covers some business investments for companies.

Bank, building societies, money markets

Interest earned is taxable in the usual way.

Growth investments, unit trusts, property

Income is taxable, as are dividends received. Capital gains are taxed as income.

Corporate Venturing Scheme

(See http://www.hmrc.gov.uk/guidance/cvs.htm)
The CVS is aimed at companies considering direct investment, in the form of a minority shareholding, in small independent higher-risk trading companies or groups of such companies. It provides tax incentives for corporate equity investment in the same types of companies as those qualifying under the Enterprise Investment Scheme (EIS) and Venture Capital Trust (VCT) scheme. The incentives are available in respect of qualifying shares issued between 1 April 2000 and 31 March 2010 (and later years). The aims of the CVS are to

- increase the availability of venture capital to small higher-risk trading companies from corporate investors, and through this
- foster wider corporate venturing relationships between otherwise unconnected companies.

The tax reliefs available are

- **investment relief** – relief against corporation tax of up to 20% of the amount subscribed for full-risk ordinary shares, provided that the shares are held throughout a qualification period
- **deferral relief** – deferral of tax on chargeable gains arising on the disposal of shares on which investment relief has been obtained and not withdrawn in full, if the gains are reinvested in new shares for which investment relief is obtained

- **loss relief** – relief against income for capital losses arising on most disposals of shares on which investment relief has been obtained and not withdrawn in full, net of the investment relief remaining after the disposal.

The investing company

The investing company must not be party to any arrangements for purchasing shares in another company which are conditional on the purchase of shares in the investing company, and throughout the qualification period must

- not own more than 30 % of the issuing company, nor be able to exercise control of the issuing company
- exist wholly for the purpose of carrying on non-financial trades, or if it is a member of a non-financial trading group of companies, exist wholly for the purpose of carrying on non-financial trades, investment (or other non-trade businesses), or be the parent company.

The issuing company

When the shares are issued the issuing company

- must be an unquoted company and must not have made any arrangements to become a quoted company
- must have gross assets of no more than £7 million immediately before, and £8 million immediately after the issue (if the issuing company is the parent company of a group, this test is applied to the group as a whole). For shares issued before 6 April 2006 the limits are £15 million before and £16 million after.

Throughout the qualification period the issuing company must not be a member of a group of companies, unless it is the parent company of the group, and must not be under the control of another company.

At least 20% of the issuing company's ordinary share capital must be held by individuals other than directors or employees (or their relatives) of an investing company, or any company connected with it.

A summary of the main rules

There are rules applying to

- the **investing company** – the company making the equity investment
- the **issuing company** – the company receiving the investment
- the **investment process** – the issue of shares to the investing company by the issuing company, and the use of the money raised by it.

A number of the rules must be satisfied throughout the 'qualification period' related to the shares. The qualification period related to the shares is a period starting with their issue and ending

- immediately before the third anniversary of the issue date where the qualifying trade for which the funds have been raised is already being carried on, or
- immediately before the third anniversary of the date on which the trade commences where the company issues the shares to raise money for a trade which is not already being carried on.

If a company is carrying on research and development from which a qualifying trade will be derived or will benefit, this activity will be treated as carrying on a qualifying trade.

Investment relief

An investing company subscribing for shares in an issuing company may claim investment relief providing certain conditions relating to both companies, and to the shares, are met. Relief is allowed against corporation tax at up to 20% of the amount subscribed.

Where investment relief is obtained, the investing company's corporation tax liability for the accounting period in which the shares were issued is reduced by whichever is the smaller of either

- 20% of the amount subscribed for the shares, or
- the amount which reduces the liability to nil.

There is no minimum amount and no absolute limit on the amount of investment relief a company can obtain on subscriptions for shares of qualifying companies.

There is CGT deferral relief and Loss relief through investing in the CVS.

Pension fund contributions

These are deductible to the company.

Maximum contribution per employee: 100% of salary up to the annual allowance of £255,000 in 2010/11. This reduces to £50,000 in 2011/12. There is a lifetime limit for each employee of £1.8 million that reduces to £1.5 million in 2011/12.

Salary Sacrifice is a recognised means to increase pension contributions. The individual tax saved and NI savings of both employer and employee can be added to the pension contribution.

Pension fund – use as a bank or purchase property

With tight monetary policy, companies may find credit unobtainable. The company or employer is able to borrow from a SSAS/SIPP 50% of value of scheme assets.

The pension fund can purchase commercial property, even from an existing director or partner owners. Rents flow in tax-free to the pension fund. When the pension fund sells the property, there is no CGT on sale of the property. Rent payments are deductible to the employer which is paying rent to the pension scheme.

If the property is made over into the pension scheme as a contribution (or series of contributions), then those 'in specie' contributions can be tax relievable to the individual (with the HMRC uplift).

On retirement, 25% of the pension fund can come to you as tax-free cash; the balance of the fund must purchase a pension or provide an income.

These types of pension funds can also make loans to an employer at up to 50% of the scheme assets.

Deferred income deposit investments

To avoid interest being paid annually, you can have a deferred deposit arrangement. For example, Zurich Bank has a product that is a bank deposit which is 100% guaranteed and in the client's name. Using an interest rate swap with a major bank, such as Barclays, the discounted interest flow is linked to an investment index chosen by the investor. Returns over 5-6 years are up to 14% annualised, with no capital loss. The business can choose when to mature the investment as corporation tax is paid in that year on the proceeds- it can also make pension contributions or expenditures that reduce taxable income in that tax year.

Entrepreneurs' relief

Entrepreneur's relief is increased to £5 million from 23.6.2010 (the previous budget increased this to £2 million), and gains above that are taxed at 10%. This would apply to an entrepreneur satisfying the criteria for relief on selling a business, and is a concession recently increased by the Government.

The entrepreneur gets an effective CGT rate of 10% on up to £5 million worth (lifetime total) of capital gains from selling a business or business share.

Entrepreneurs' relief and family company shares

The relief will have effect for gains on disposals of shares in a trading company provided that throughout a one-year qualifying period before you sell your shares you:

- are an officer or employee of the company, or of a company in the same group of companies;
- own at least 5% of the ordinary share capital of the company and that holding enables you to exercise at least 5% of the voting rights in that company.
- where the company (or group) does not cease to trade, the one-year qualifying period is the year ending on the date the shares or securities are disposed of.
- where the company (or group) ceases to trade before the disposal of the shares or securities, the one-year qualifying period ends on the date trading ceased, and the disposal must be made within three years of the date of cessation.

Director's loan accounts and Partner/LLP capital accounts

Directors usually invest in their own businesses through introducing capital to the company. This need not be cash, and could be assets. The company can pay interest on the money, which is taxable in the hands of the director. The director could draw down tax free 'income' from this arrangement (a return of his own capital), as this is his money loaned to the business. However, the director's loan account does not qualify for BPR (business property reliefs) and will be subject to inheritance taxes, a fact often overlooked by directors. It would be a better arrangement to arrange a for loan finance with a bank and to repay the director's loan account so that it can be IHT tax-sheltered. The bank interest would be deductible to the company and reduce the tax on its profits. Partners and LLP members invest in their businesses through capital accounts. They do get BPR relief for inheritance tax purposes, (unlike directors in companies) as these accounts are seen to be part of the business itself. Interest can be paid on the capital account, which is taxable. If they could withdraw a capital account – in terms of their partnership agreement – and replace it with bank finance then this is a way to get capital out of the business pre-retirement.

Businesses can create tax efficiency through available allowances and expense deductions. Some investments like the CVS are tax reducing, whereas investments such as contributions in to pension funds reduce taxable profits. Many businesses have many thousands of pounds lying idle in money markets or at call, earning miserly rates of interest. If the business decided when it required capital (for example to purchase machinery), and the time for which it could invest, it could increase its returns substantially. Businesses are losing out through poor investment returns, and the lack of investment opportunity.

14

Investing in Property

There are many different ways to invest into property – you can be a passive or an active investor. The passive investor will purchase funds in a property unit trust or investment trust, or an investment bond; the active investor will explore options to purchase a property and make a capital gain from the investor. Investments can be made in the UK or offshore, and holiday properties would be included here.

Investments can be into residential or commercial property, which can be held for the investor or rented out. Some ways are tax-efficient, others are not. However, many people feel more secure when investing into bricks and mortar, as even with falls in property prices, the basic asset still remains – unless destroyed by one of life's catastrophes such as earthquake or fire. Protecting the property is there an important aspect, and property should always be insured.

Passive investors

Investing into commercial property is once again attracting large inflows of funds. However, it wasn't so long ago that the property market slumped (by 2009 – from 2007- it had, on average fallen by over 45% – the IPD UK property index was at -45% in 2009 and has recovered to – 35% in 2010). During the period of slump, property, being an illiquid investment, was subject to suspension of the funds, causing great inconvenience to investors. Conversely, there were bargains to be had, as property developers failed to meet bank covenants, or ran out of money. However, caution is still urged with the property market.

Commercial property receives returns from capital growth and from rental yields. The more costly the price of property, the lower the rental return yields. Choosing the best fund is therefore crucial to your property portfolio.

There is now a potential for good returns where invested in good quality commercial property. Some feel that returns are artificially high because of the influx of investor's cash, and funds sitting on cash mountains that need to be invested, which drives up value and reduces returns from rentals. Property could be seen to be expensive, and may become priced too high.

Strong fund managers with good selections and tenancy rates, low void rates, good average returns, tenants with long leases – funds like Threadneedle, Aviva, SWIP, Henderson and L & G, Aberdeen and others all offer good potential. Fund managers will invest in UK as well as overseas property for the best deals.

The major risk for property funds is that of liquidity – the inability to turn the investment into cash, should you wish to get out of it. However, property is one of the major asset classes and essential to have some of your diversified money in this sector.

Tax

Property funds can be held by ISAs, where the gains are tax-free. Similarly for pension funds. For unit trusts and investment trusts and OEICs, capital gains may be subject to capital gains tax (after your CGT allowance) and income received as dividends will be subject to dividend taxation if not a basic rate taxpayer.

Direct property investment

More active investors have a number of options to consider. Firstly, the excitement of investing into and managing a property and its tenants is a business for some people, whilst for others it is a one-off investment, for example when you purchase your own home.

Own home

The average house price as at 7th October 2010 (BBC News Channel) is £230,562, broken down as follows:

Detached	£328,778
Semi-Detached	£199,475
Terrace	£186,74
Flat	£219,033

Obviously there are regional fluctuations in pricing. What is important to note is that the barriers to entry for new or first time buyers, remains beyond reach, unless there is parental help or other funds available for a deposit. Obtaining a mortgage has also been very difficult, with combined incomes required of over £50,000 to purchase just the average priced house, and substantial deposits required.

However, for the investor, after a fall in house values during the downturn 2007 – 2009, values have started to creep up again and the annual change in house prices (October 2009 to October 2010 has been 22.9%). Don't rely on surging values as the last quarter (June to September 2010, the index fell by -1.8%. Housing remained the UK's most valuable asset – up £126 billion or 3.2% to £4.05 trillion over the year and accounting for 61% of the country's net worth. (*The Independent* 2nd August 2010.)

Be prepared to pay search, title deeds and conveyancing fees to transfer the property to you, as well as estate agent's commission.

Tax

When you purchase your house, you may have to pay SDLT – Stamp Duty Land Tax- which is determined by a sliding scale according to value.

Value up to £125,000	Nil
Over £125,000 – £250,000	1%
	(but relief for first time buyers at nil)
Over £250,000 – £500,000	3%
Over £500,000	4%

If you own then sell your principal private residence, there is no capital gains tax to pay. If you gift your private residence to another there may be inheritance tax to pay in advance at 20% if the gift is worth over £325,000 (the nil rate band), and a further 20% (tapered) if you do not survive for 7 years. If you gift your principal residence to another (or to a trust) but stay in the property without paying commercial rent, this could be a gift with reservation, where the PET rules do not apply and the house is inheritance taxable, and you may also be liable to an income tax charge. On death, the value of the house could be subject to inheritance tax if over the nil rate band.

Ownership can be singly or jointly with another (need not be a spouse or civil partner), and held jointly or as tenants in common. If held as joint owners, then on death of one of the owners, the full ownership of the property reverts to the survivor. If held as tenants in common, then each owner can pass his or her share to whomsoever they wish.

Rent-a-room relief – if you rent out a room in your house to a lodger, the first £4,250 is tax-free. Rent-a-room applies only to owner occupiers and tenants who receive rent from letting furnished accommodation in their only or main home. If your gross receipts (before expenses and including any amounts received for meals, goods and services provided, such as cleaning or laundry) and any balancing charges do not exceed £4,250 you will be exempt from Income Tax on any profits made. You can however, opt out of Rent-a-room; you may want to do this if you have made a loss. HMRC states (Helpsheet 223) that If your gross receipts are more than £4,250 you can choose between paying tax on:

your actual profit (gross rents minus actual expenses and capital allowances)

or gross receipts (and any balancing charges) minus £4,250 – with no deduction for expenses or capital allowances.

Rent-a-room relief applies to a tax year and the limit of £4,250 is reduced to £2,125 if during the basis period someone else received income from letting accommodation in the same property.

Rent-a-room does not apply to income from accommodation used as an office or for business other than by genuine lodgers (for example, students who are provided with study facilities in their lodgings, or lodgers who do some work in your home in the evenings or weekends).

Also check with your household insurance company that you can rent out a room in your house.

Expenses related to premises

You can deduct the costs of maintaining your business premises – including rent, rates, heat, light, repairs and insurance. You can also deduct the business part of these costs if you run your business from home.

If you run a business from home and are claiming business expenses for doing so, part of your home may become subject to capital gains tax if you sell it. It is wise to cease the business before selling to regain the non business status for a private residence.

Mortgages

Funding the purchase of your property can be made through a cash purchase, house swap (often developers wish to sell a property but can't do so and will take your property in part-exchange); or through taking up a mortgage. The old days of interest only mortgages have more or less disappeared – expect to have a repayment mortgage, where you pay back capital and interest payments. The shorter the mortgage period, the more expensive the repayments will be, but in the long run, the less interest you will pay. If you can get a fortnightly payment mortgage, you will save thousands in interest payments. However, this concept is largely unknown to UK mortgage providers – but shop around. Expect to pay a deposit of at least 25% – however, some lenders will go now to 95% and even 100% mortgages. Mortgages are really about pricing and what you can afford. Mortgages are worked out as a multiple of your income, for example, 3 times a single income or 4.5 times a joint income. So if earning £50,000 between a couple, expect a mortgage of around £225,000.

Definitely shop around for the best mortgage deal. Bank interest rates may be low now but could increase in the future. You may decide to have a tracker mortgage (which tracks the bank rate or some other index), or to fix your mortgage payments for a period, so that the repayments are certain and you can budget for them. If possible, and employed (this doesn't work for the self-employed), get payment protection insurance if you are made redundant or become seriously ill, so that your mortgage payments can be kept up and you do not lose your house. Also consider life assurance and critical illness cover to enable your mortgage to be paid off on death or if you have a critical illness. No one wants to leave their family without a roof over their heads if catastrophe strikes.

Buying a property for a student

The investor has three main routes to consider. Firstly, to purchase a property and then to rent it out for rental income to provide for school and university fees.

The second option is primarily for university students, where the parent or the student purchases a property to live in (thus saving on accommodation fees), and rents rooms out to other students to part pay for fees. Both of the above may involve a mortgage loan and other capital invested and will have maintenance and management expenses, as well as the possibility of capital gains tax payable on sale, if not a primary residence. The student could be a 'property manager' collecting rents and managing the property whilst living there – and receive a fee for doing so. Council tax is also generally not paid so long as all are students living in the rented accommodation. However, if one of the tenants is not a student, then council tax is payable by all of them.

The third option is where an investment is made into a property fund or portfolio, producing income or interest that can be used for school and university fees. Income returns on commercial property investments are possibly up to 5% gross, but this cannot be guaranteed.

Some investors prefer fixed property investments as these have a lower volatility factor in terms of risk than say equities, for example. However, this is not always the case and properties between 2007 and 2009 lost substantial value (whilst rental streams may not have suffered).

An example could be a commercial property investment of say £300,000 providing income at, say, 5%, which is £15,000 gross per annum.

Property owning trusts can stream income to beneficiaries to be used for school fees. Property owning companies can do the same for shareholders. However, both require careful financial and legal planning to avoid the Settlor (in the case of a trust, the person setting it up), and the parent (in the case of the company) being taxed instead of the child beneficiary or shareholder. Your strategy is to ensure that a new company is established with minors from the outset, with realistic shareholdings purchased with cash donated by a grandparent or third party. Children are taxpayers in their own right, with personal allowances – currently the first £6,475 is not taxable (2010/11 tax year). Dividends received by the children should be paid directly to the school or university by them, not by their parents.

Buy to let

Here the investor purchases one or more properties with the intention of letting them out, to gain from rental incomes (which are offset against mortgage interest for tax purposes), and capital value increases in the long term. One of the best websites with answers is www.thisismoney.co.uk/buy-to-let-tips where you can get tips on where to find out more about buy to let. Their top ten tips summarised are:

1. Research the market

To ensure that this is the right investment for you. Can your money perform better elsewhere? You may be tying up money that you cannot access, and values may fall.

If you know someone who has entered the buy-to-let market, ask them about their experiences.

2. Choose a promising area

Promising does not mean most expensive or cheapest. What has special appeal? Where are the good schools for young families? Where do the students want to live?

3. Do the maths

Establish costs of houses, and likely rents. You will need to cover costs from income. Buy-to-let lenders want rent to cover 125% of the mortgage repayments, although many had relaxed this in recent years. Many are now demanding 25%+ deposits, or even larger (some up to 60%), with mortgage rates considerably above residential mortgage deals. The best rate buy-to-let mortgages also come with large arrangement fees.

Will your investment work out? Can you afford any months where you don't have a tenant?

4. Shop around

If you are looking for advice consider using a specialist buy-to-let mortgage broker.

5. Think about your target tenant

Who are they and what do they want? If they are students, it needs to be easy to clean and comfortable but not luxurious. If they are young professionals it should be modern and stylish but not overbearing.

6. Don't be over ambitious

Rent should be the key return for buy-to-let. You need to build up a rent reserve to pay off the mortgage in the long term, or have a further deposit for further buy to let investments.

7. Consider looking further afield

The best investment could be in a town further away from you.

8. Haggle over price

As a buy-to-let investor you have the same advantage as a first-time buyer when it comes to negotiating a discount.

9. Know the pitfalls

Before you make any investment you should always investigate the negative aspects as well as the positive. What if house prices fall, or you do not have tenants? Can you afford to continue?

10. Consider how hands-on you want to be

If you use an agent to manage your property this costs 10%-15% of the rental income, or do it yourself. Do you have the time and resources to do so? You may need to build up plumber, builder and other contacts to maintain your property.

Overall at present, this is a tough time for buy to let. However, there are bargains to be had and yields are typically 5%-7% for better propositions.

If investors are willing to accept that the value of their property may slide in the short term, and ensure their property meets the criteria of at least 75% to 85% loan-to-value and returning 125% of monthly mortgage payments then it can continue to be a good long-term investment.

A typical example may be if aiming at rental income delivering at least 20% above mortgage costs. If landlord mortgage rates are at 5.49% (3 year fixed rate), and your deposit is £50,000 and you borrow £100,000, your monthly interest-only payments would come to £457, generating a £343 monthly profit from a £800 rent.

Even if that £343 was not defrayed by other costs, such as maintenance, it would still make a yearly return of only 5.49% on your £50,000 capital.

There is plenty of information available for investors through the internet, or you can obtain regular tips and tax strategies from 'Landlords Insider Secrets' newsletter – tips on how to end a tenancy etc at http://tinyurl.com/35g4mob to read the newsletter, or email amer@taxinsider.co.uk for more information.

Tax issues

The sale of your investment property may be subject to capital gains tax, and the amount payable depends on whether you hold the property in your own name, or through a trust, company or pension fund. There are CGT reliefs, such as holdover reliefs available, or personal exemptions, or trust exemptions from CGT. There is no CGT payable if the gain arises within a pension fund.

Certain costs, such as management costs and interest on your mortgage (not the capital element) are deductible for income tax purposes. Capital expenditure would not be deductible to you, but allowances may be available to you. Rental income is taxable. There are many tax strategies available to reduce the incidence of taxation, including loss reliefs. If you deal in properties, as opposed to merely investing and then selling, then income derived is subject to income tax, not capital gains tax.

If you let out property you can deduct certain expenses and tax allowances from your rental income to work out your taxable profit (or loss). If you have several UK residential lettings you pool the income and expenses together. But you work out holiday letting and overseas letting profits separately.

Allowable expenses

The expenses you can deduct from letting income (unless it's under the Rent-a-room scheme) include:

letting agent's fees; legal fees for lets of a year or less, or for renewing a lease for less than 50 years; accountant's fees ; buildings and contents insurance; interest on property loans; maintenance and repairs to the property (but not improvements); utility bills (like gas, water, electricity); rent, ground rent, service charges; Council Tax; services you pay for, like cleaning or gardening; other direct costs of letting the property, like phone calls, stationery, advertising.

If your annual income from the letting for the tax year 2009-10 is less than £68,000 (before you've taken off expenses) you include the total expenses on your tax return; if it's £68,000 or over you need to provide a breakdown.

Bear in mind that you can only claim expenses that are solely for running your property letting business. If the expense is only partly for running your business (or if you use the property yourself) then you may only be able to claim part of it.

Non-allowable expenses

When you work out your profit, you can't deduct:

- 'capital' costs, like furniture or the property itself
- personal expenses – costs that aren't to do with your letting business
- any loss you make when you sell the property

But you may be able to claim some allowances instead.

Allowances that can reduce your taxable profit

There are different types of allowance you may be able to claim for your capital costs. Capital costs include expenditure you make on assets like furniture and machinery. The allowances you can claim for some of your capital costs vary according to the type of letting.

Commercial property in pension funds

A pension fund (SIPP or SSAS, for example) may own a commercial property, and can even purchase it from you. There are no 'connecting rules' prohibiting this type of transaction – even though there used to be in the past. The pension fund can borrow up to 50% of its scheme assets by value, and can also enter into mortgage loans and pay interest. Rental income from letting out the property is not taxed in the pension fund (and may be deductible to the tenant); there is no capital gains on sale of the property from the pension fund. You can set your own level of returns for the pension fund dependant on the rental income flow. This is a very tax-efficient way of holding property. The investor could tax shelter his commercial property in his pension fund and at the time that he requires a pension, can purchase the property himself or sell it to a third party, or even leave it in the pension fund to continue to produce income.

Furnished holiday lettings

You may have purchased or wish to purchase a second holiday home and to rent it out to tenants for income, when not in use by you. If you let out a furnished holiday home in the UK or elsewhere in the European Economic Area (EEA), your rental income may be treated differently for tax purposes from other rental income. However, your property must keep to some rules known as 'qualifying tests'. Current rules for furnished holiday lettings (See HMRC – www.direct.gov.uk for further information) are that it must be:

In the UK or EEA (see more in the section 'If the property is in the European Economic Area'); furnished; available for commercial letting to the public, as holiday accommodation, for at least 140 days a year; commercially let as holiday accommodation for at least 70 days a year (the rent must be charged at market rate – not at cheap rates to friends and family); a short term letting of no more than 31 days.

Lets to the same person

You can let to the same person more than once as long as each let is less than 31 days. All of these lets together can total more than 31 days and still count as furnished holiday lettings.

Lets for periods longer than 31 days

You can let the property out for periods longer than 31 days in one stretch but none of the days will count towards your qualification. This is known as 'longer term occupation'. However if the total of all or any 'longer term occupation' lets' is more than 155 days in the tax year, your property will no longer qualify as a furnished holiday letting. If your property doesn't qualify as a furnished holiday letting, you will be taxed under the residential property lettings rules. If the property is in the European Economic Area from 22 April 2009 HM Revenue & Customs (HMRC) has applied a temporary extension of the current rules to UK taxpayers with property outside of the UK but within the EEA to choose whether they wish to be taxed under: the furnished holiday letting rules – if the property qualifies; the normal rules for property businesses; and that these arrangements will continue to apply for the 2010-11 tax year (the 2010 financial year for Corporation Tax).

Tax

Your profit on furnished holiday lettings is worked out in the same way as for other rental income, except that you claim 'capital allowances' rather than the 'wear and tear' allowance.

Examples of expenses that qualify for capital allowances include the cost of furnishings and furniture, and equipment such as refrigerators and washing machines.

If you sell or 'otherwise dispose' of the property

You may be able to take advantage of Capital Gains Tax reliefs, such as 'Business Asset Roll-Over Relief'. For example, if you reinvest the sale proceeds within three years in certain other business assets, you may be able to defer payment of Capital Gains Tax until you dispose of those new assets.

If you make a loss

If your business is run on a commercial basis any loss can be offset against your other income, not just the property income, reducing your overall tax bill. Or you can carry the loss forward and offset it against future letting profits

You need to declare your rental income from furnished holiday lettings using the land and property pages of your Self Assessment tax return. If you don't receive one automatically, follow the link below to find out how to get one. You should also use the same property pages of your tax return to declare income from furnished holiday lettings property in the EEA.

UK and overseas furnished residential lettings

For furniture and equipment provided with a furnished residential letting (excluding furnished holiday lettings) you can claim a 'wear and tear' allowance. The allowance is 10 per cent of the 'net rent' – this being the rent received less any costs you pay that a tenant would usually pay.

As an alternative to the wear and tear allowance, you can claim a 'renewals' allowance. This covers the cost of replacing furniture or equipment, including small items like cutlery. To work it out, take the cost of the replacement item and deduct from it:

- the amount you sold the old one for (if you got anything for it)
- anything extra you paid for a better one

Once you've chosen which of these allowances to claim for a property, you can't switch between them from year to year.

Furnished holiday lettings

If you own a qualifying furnished holiday letting in the UK or in the European Economic Area you can claim a 'capital allowance' for the cost of each item of furniture and equipment you provide with the property. Or you can claim a renewals allowance (explained above). You can't claim wear and tear allowances.

Once you make a choice for each item, you must keep to it.

All letting properties

Whatever the type of letting, you can claim a capital allowance on the cost of things that you need for running your property letting business, like cleaning and gardening equipment. You can also claim for equipment that isn't for the use of a single let property, like a boiler that heats more than one property.

How much capital allowance can you claim?

The allowance depends on what you buy. You can usually claim 50 per cent of the cost when you buy it – but sometimes 100 per cent for some environmentally friendly expenditure. Each year after that you can claim 25 per cent of what's left. HM Revenue & Customs (HMRC) changes the percentages from time to time. The allowance is deducted along with other expenses in calculating your profits.

You'll get smaller allowances if you use the item privately or for anything other than your business.

Which year do expenses belong to?

You have to allocate expenses to the year they apply to – it doesn't matter when you actually pay them. Sometimes you may have to allocate part of an expense to one year and part to another.

Losses

Normally, if your letting business makes a loss, you can carry it forward to a later year and offset it against your future profits from the same business. If it's a UK holiday letting business you can offset your loss against all of your other income, not just your property income, for years up to and including 2010/11.

For further information see www.direct.gov.uk in respect of taxes on property and what is allowable and what is taxable.

Purchasing offshore property

This is a specialised and often complex area, where local knowledge is required. If a UK tax resident then the same rules away to second properties, whether offshore or in the UK. Local jurisdictions will also have their rules. For example, it may be better to purchase your holiday property or second home through a trust or a company, than owning it outright in your name, as this may escape foreign taxes.

It is possible to raise a mortgage on your UK property to purchase abroad.

Holiday Property Bond

This is an investment into an Isle of Man investment bond that entitles you to stay in a holiday property in the UK and abroad, and in properties maintained at a very high standard. As part of lifestyle planning you may wish to invest into future holidays for life, and for future generations. With over 36,000 investors, the Bond is a life assurance bond investing, after initial charges, in properties and securities. Properties are booked for a no profit 'user charge' and points issued with the Bond. There is a quarterly fee of around twenty-five pounds including VAT linked to RPI, with all other management fees paid from securities. Investment is from £4,000. Encashment may be made under the terms of the 'Holiday Satisfaction Guaranteed' offer. Otherwise you may encash after two years at a value linked to that of the properties and securities but you may not see a profit and may incur a loss because of initial charges and fluctuations in asset values. In exceptional circumstances encashment may be deferred for up to twelve months. No medical examination is required for investors.

As a Holiday Property Bondholder, your interests are further protected by HSBC Trustee (Guernsey) Limited – to whom all cheques are made payable, and who control all the fund's assets. Financial Services Regulation – the sale of Holiday Property Bond is authorised and regulated by the Financial Services Authority.

Distressed properties and rent back – sale and leaseback

There are businesses that will buy your property from you and allow you to remain in the property, usually at a reduced rent. Beware – some of these have failed to honour their 'guarantees' and the original homeowners (who usually sold up because they were in debt, or to release equity) have lost their homes.

Releasing property equity

You may release capital from either your own residence or a second property through what is known as equity release, through either a mortgage or remortgage, or a lifetime mortgage or reversion scheme, and use the capital generally for any purpose. Capital released in this way is not taxable in your hands (as it is considered a loan). Interest payable is not deductible to the primary principal homeowner (unless used to purchase shares in a company or a share of a partnership), but may be deductible as an expense for an investment property, where capital is raised to use a deposit to purchase another property, for example. Remember that any loans where interest or capital is repayable must be properly serviced, or you could lose your property or asset.

This chapter has described many different forms of property investment, from the passive investor, to the more active investor. Returns from property investment can be good and consistent – one only has to look at the student accommodation sector, for example. Brandeaux operates a student fund that consistently returns 9%-10% per annum, even in bad economic times. The Property Bourse has strategies to leverage your investment for above average returns, and many property developers are producing good results for their investors. Others have not fared as well, and it is important to do your homework, and to seek professional advice before acting.

15

Other Investments: Hard Assets

This chapter deals with investments such as hard assets, antique furniture, stamp collections, wine and gold. The usual rule when disposing of an asset is that it may be subject to capital gains tax, unless it is exempt.

Reliefs and exemptions

An individual is entitled to the following reliefs and exemptions:

Your capital gain is the difference between the price you originally paid for the asset (or if it was given to you – what it was worth on that day) and the amount you get when you sell it. However there are a number of special rules to bear in mind and these are listed below.

The first £10,100 of your gains for 2010/11 is free from tax – this is called your annual exemption.

A husband and wife (or civil partners) each receive an annual exemption.

You do not need to tell the Revenue about any capital gains if they are less than the annual exemption of £10,100 and the proceeds after costs are less than £40,400 for 2010/11. This last figure is always four times the annual exemption and changes from year to year.

If your gains are more than £10,100, you will need to complete a tax return to show the capital gain you have made. If you do not normally complete a return you will only be expected to do so If you give an asset to your husband or wife whilst you are legally married and living together – you will not pay any CGT at that time. The same rules apply to a civil partnership.

One of the exemptions is the chattel test.

The following assets are free from capital gains tax: (as exempt)

- Private motor cars
- Gifts to charities
- Some Government Securities
- Personal belongings where sale proceeds are less than £6,000
- Prizes and betting winnings
- Gifts of cash
- Assets held in ISAs
- Foreign currency for your own use
- Sale of principal private residence

Chattels (assets bought and sold for less than £6,000)

Any gain is exempt from Capital Gains tax if the asset is bought and sold for less than £6,000. If there are joint owners, such as husband and wife or civil partners, each has a separate £6,000 limit to use in connection with their share of the asset in question.

If the sale proceeds are more than £6,000, the gain cannot be more than: (Proceeds of sale x 5/3) less £6,000.

So for example if you sold a table £7,200 in October 2010 having bought the chest for £4,570 in July 2010 – the gain is £7,200 – 4,570 = £2,630 but it is restricted to (5/3 x (7,200-6,000)) = £2,000

If the asset is sold at a loss for less than £6,000, you have to treat the sales proceeds as being £6,000 for working out any allowable capital loss. For example if you have a painting that cost £12,000 and you sell it for £5,000, it would be treated as being sold for £6,000 giving an allowable loss of £5,000 and not £7,000 as might be expected.

Collections

If the assets comprise a set or collection they are treated as separate assets unless they are sold to the same person or someone who is connected with or related to that person in which case the sales are added together for the purposes of the £6,000 exemption.

A set or collection is where the assets are essentially similar or complimentary and their value taken together is higher than if they were look at individually.

If you sell a set to someone you are connected with over more than one tax year the gain is worked out just as for a set or collection but is then a proportion of the gain is allocated to the year of each sale.

Antique furniture, stamp collections, classic cars, paintings

If you are seen to be trading in any of the above, then you could be liable to income tax on your profits. However, as a collector and engaging in one-off sales, you may be liable to capital gains tax, unless exempt (motor cars) or exempt under the chattel rules or wasting assets rules (see below under wine). If so, your enjoyment or hobby will prove to be a tax shelter for you. Even if not exempt, the CGT allowance is £10,100 and could cover most disposals.

Wine

Investment into fine wines can be tax-free and also act as a tax shelter. There is no capital gains tax on the sale, as wine is considered to have a life expectancy of less than 50 years, a wasting asset attaining a chattel status which allows avoidance of capital gains penalties on re-sale. Individuals must not be seen to be buying and selling wine in a controlled fashion as they are likely to be deemed as trading and as such profits would be subject to income tax. So, avoid trading status, use the wasting asset or chattels exemptions, keep records for self-assessment and make full disclosure on your tax return.

You can enjoy tax-free profits whilst your investment steadily appreciates in value.

If profits made on wine sales are within capital gains tax rather than trading transactions, the taxpayer can enjoy the benefits of taper relief, the annual exemption and most importantly, potential total exemption due to the following possible reliefs:

- wasting asset exemption (TCGA 1992 s45)
- chattels exemption (TCGA 1992 s262)

It is these two reliefs that merit consideration in the context of wine investment,

Wasting asset exemption

TCGA 1992 s44 (1) defines a "wasting asset" as being an asset with a predictable life not exceeding fifty years. It then goes on to state that "life", in relation to any tangible moveable property, means useful life, having regard to the purpose for which the tangible assets were acquired or provided by the person making the disposal;

Section 45 (1) then goes on to state that no chargeable gain shall accrue on the disposal of an asset which is both tangible moveable property and a wasting asset. Clearly it is in the interest therefore of the wine investor making a gain on disposal to demonstrate that the wine had a useful life of fifty years or less.

Chattels exemption

If it has to be accepted that the wine does not fall within the wasting assets exemption, it may still be possible to utilise the chattels exemption relief. Where a chattel is sold for proceeds of less than £6,000, s262 TCGA 1992 states that a chargeable gain will not arise. Clearly the objective behind this exemption is to prevent a taxpayer having to make detailed calculations every time any small asset is disposed of. However, it may assist the wine investor who is making small scale disposals. (Source Richard Holme and Claire Appleton, Creaseys Tax Consulting, Tunbridge Wells)

Gold

In the UK, gold coin trading is VAT free, and gold coins that are legal currency within the UK (Britannias and sovereigns) are also free of capital gains tax. Foreign gold coins (such as Krugerrands) are not free of CGT. People and pension funds can buy gold bullion as investments. Otherwise you can invest into funds that invest in gold mining and gold itself.

The 2006 Budget, permitted investment-grade gold bullion to be included in Self Invested Personal Pensions [SIPPs]. These popular government approved schemes allow individuals greater control over the investments within their pension funds.

Gold has increased significantly in value against sterling recently – in the past six years, and investor interest continues to thrive. With growing public concerns about mainstream investments, gold bullion is increasingly seen as a sound portfolio diversifier.

Buying investment grade gold bullion for investment is stamp duty free and tax-free (VAT exempt) in the UK and EU due to the EU Gold Directive of 2000.

Gold bullion is allowed in a SIPP providing it is investment grade gold which is gold of a purity not less than 995 thousandths or 99.5% pure and which is in the form of a bar, or of a wafer, of a weight accepted by the bullion markets. The bullion must be immoveable and stored with a secure third party. It cannot be taken possession of and used as a "pride in possession" article. Thus ETFs, some digital gold providers, allocated gold accounts and gold certificates are all allowed in the new SIPP.

Collective investment vehicles are a good way to invest in the precious metal mining sector as an investor's risk is reduced; mutual funds are not dependent on the performance and profits of one or two individual gold mining company and specialists in the field choose a portfolio of gold mining companies.

16

Tax Strategies in Financial Planning

It is beyond the scope of this book to deal in any depth with tax strategies that do not involve investments, of which there are many. Ways to save SDLT, VAT and other taxes are the preserve of tax consultants. Yet, there are many ways to make investments more tax-efficient, and in this way to create substantial savings for investors, whilst at the same preserving capital for you and future generations. Whilst tax planning is carried out throughout the tax year, much of it is bunched for attention at the tax year-end.

Individuals

Individuals should assess what taxes they are and will be liable for and whether they wish to get tax back from a previous tax year. This may influence which investments they make and why. The main season for ISAs, VCTs and EIS investments, as well as pensions is in the final three months of the tax year. Product providers, who have not already made market offerings, will certainly wish to bring their products to market to catch the year-end sales. One can expect at least 15-20 VCTs and EIS products to choose from, and this is the final tax year for an EZ investment.

Individuals must ask themselves the question as to whether they are utilising all allowances and exemptions for them and their families. How efficient is their investment portfolio? When was it last reviewed? Can they do better. Most would like to see a better return coupled with tax savings where possible.

Businesses

There are numerous tax strategies that businesses can use. The sole trader usually uses individual tax –reducing and tax-free investments, such as pensions. However, the individual sole trader can also use capital allowances, for example.

All businesses will be looking to reduce tax, cut costs and increase profits.

If you are self employed, either a sole trader or in partnership, you are approaching a key date – the end of yet another tax year.

Due to the current economic downturn you may recently have experienced a drop in your profitability, indeed you may be trading at a loss.

For example, timing of capital purchases or disposals, either before or after the end of the tax year, can be organised to maximise claims under the new Annual Investment Allowance of £100,000. If your profits have decreased this year, to 31 March 2011, compared to the previous year (31 March 2010), this may reduce the tax payments on account you offer in January and July 2011.

If you are forced to lay off staff and have some flexibility when you make redundancy payments, is this best charged in this current year, or the decision deferred to the next trading year?

What is your bad debt situation? Have you made adequate provision in your accounts? Has any VAT on bad debts over 6 months old been claimed back? Please note that if you use Cash Accounting for VAT you only pay VAT added to your invoices when you are paid – so you don't need to worry about claiming for bad debts.

If you have made a loss in this current year does this affect the tax relief you may have received on pension contributions? Will the tax have to be repaid or contributions recovered?

How is the business's cash invested? Can it be bettered? Do you have an investment plan for when cash is required? For example, you may have set aside money to buy a new factory five years hence, but the money is invested in the money markets at very low interest rates.

Payments on account for 2010/11

Unless you make a specific request to reduce the amount due, your payments on account for 2010/11 will be based on your actual payments for the previous year, 2009/10. If you have prepared management accounts to the end of December 2010 you should be able to estimate your likely results for 2010/11. If they are lower than the previous year's results you can ask for the payments on account to be reduced. And don't forget, your taxable profits include deductions for capital expenditure. From the 1 April 2010 certain expenditures qualify for a 100% write off up to a maximum of £100,000.

This is fairly basic tax planning that can be overlooked.

Trusts

Trustees need to review their investments and the purpose of these investments, as well as the type of trusts that they are trustees of. Can they be made more efficient, do they have an up- to -date Policy Statement and Guidelines (PSG) which is their investment plan? Are the trustees paying too much tax? Should investments be diversified? How can the trustees create more income for life tenants and capital for remaindermen? All of these questions should be answered in the quest for greater efficiency.

Overall

This is a good opportunity for a financial and investment review, taking into account all your circumstances. You may need to pay a fee for this service, using a certified or chartered financial planner with the necessary expertise to help you.

17

Bringing Your Plan Together

Some readers will only be interested in specific investments, others will wish to plan an investment strategy, and ensure that the correct investments are selected for or by them to suit their particular circumstances, and objectives.

The following steps will help you to decide on your *investment strategy*:

1. List your current assets and investments. Include the amounts invested, the term of the investment, the status of the investment as to taxable, tax-free, tax reducing or tax deferred. Include the proposed returns, such as a current interest rate on a fixed deposit.

2. List your current liabilities and the payment details. Include the term of the liability and monthly interest payments. Can you do better? Often a good investment is to pay off a debt that has a high interest rate (usually higher than that offered by a bank or building society investment) – this saves you money.

3. Consider your investment risk profile for different situations. Your risk profile may be different for investments, pension funding, taking out a mortgage to purchase a property, for example.

4. Note your tax status. Are you a non taxpayer, basic rate taxpayer, higher rate taxpayer, or additional rate taxpayer.

5. Can you include your spouse, partner, or family members in your investment decision- making? Using other people's tax exemptions and tax status to ensure you earn more for your investment money, is a wise move.

6. List your aims and objectives. These may include, for example, to fund for university fees for one child from 2012 to 2015 at a cost of £12,000 per annum; or to have an emergency fund of at least 3 months wages; or to save for a round the world holiday; or to get the best returns from your investment money and to research the best way to do this. You may wish to supplement your retirement income, and are at the limit of allowable pension funding. What alternative tax-efficient investments are there?

7. Either complete a personal financial plan yourself or have a certified or chartered financial planner do one for you. It could be that you have an inheritance tax problem and any future investments need to be ring-fenced to protect them from IHT. Money spent now on a good financial plan can save you thousands later.

8. Are your will(s) consistent with your planning? Do you have enough liquidity in your estate (cash) to meet liabilities such as IHT and to make bequests or leave legacies, or sums in trust? This brings out the importance of the '4 Pillar Philosophy' that your money should be strictly spent in accordance with your need requirements and objectives, which are properly prioritised. It is no good investing money for retirement when you haven't considered the basics first – protection of family, health, emergency fund, then retirement and investments. Or perhaps these prioritisations are not as important to you, and you wish to make best use of tax allowable investments. The choice is yours.

9. The choice of what and where to invest is important. Your tax status and overall asset position will help you with your decision-making. For example, you may have an IHT problem and making investments such as ISAs, term deposits, unit trusts, property could make it worse. Imagine losing 40% of the value of your assets on death, having spent years in building them up? Instead you could have considered investments that mitigate IHT or fall out of your estate to be preserved for your heirs, such as a discounted gift trust investment bond, or an EIS investment. Alternatively, you may need instant access to your investments, and tying them up for long periods may involve you in penalties if you cash them in too early, or the loss of interest and returns.

10. Whilst saving or reducing tax should not be an overriding reason to invest, it does influence the investor. If paying tax at 40% or 50% on income and 32.5% and 42.5% on dividends, if certain investments reduce your tax or are tax-free then they must be considered. With very low interest rates on bank and building society investments, after tax, the amount received could be negligible, and this is reduced further in real terms by the effects of inflation on your money. You may also fall foul of tax traps such as the age-related allowance of £22,900 where your personal allowance at age 65 and over is reduced on a one pound for two pounds basis, and at any age for the personal allowance over £100,000. For example:

- *If you are 65 or over and your income is between £22,900 and £100,000*
  If your income is over £22,900 (the income limit for age-related allowances) but not more than £100,000, your age-related Personal Allowance is reduced by half of the amount – £1 for every £2 – you have over the £22,900 limit, until the basic rate allowance is reached. So if, for example, you're 66 and have income of £23,400 – £500 over the limit – your age-related Personal Allowance is reduced by £250 to £9,240.

- *If your income is above £100,000*
  From the tax year 2010-11, if your income is over £100,000, your Personal Allowance is reduced by half of the amount – £1 for every £2 – you have over that limit. If your income is large enough, your Personal Allowance will be reduced to nil. This £100,000 limit applies *irrespective* of your age.

If the income from investments was tax-free, or you were using your CGT allowance to take gains tax-free, then the age allowance traps could be avoided. Careful planning is required.

The same is the case if you are being means-tested for benefits. Additional income or investments made by you could mean that you no longer qualify for certain benefits. This could extend to care home fees for example, and what the local council or authority will pay for your care.

Adopting the correct approach

The investment arena is vast. Every financial adviser will not know about all of the available investments in the market place. Many may not even be able to advise you on certain investments, as they do not carry the necessary authorisations to do so. It is unlikely that the average investor will truly maximise his or her position in respect of being most tax-efficient, earning the best returns, providing the highest income, protecting assets, avoiding the tax traps, on their own. Most will require some help or assistance, from tax advisers, investment and financial planners. The best this book can do is to point you in the right direction. What is important is to ensure that you have a diversified approach to investments, with the correct asset allocation, and that you only take up investments within your risk profile. This is the general position. For those with spare cash (which they can afford to lose) who would prefer a more risky investment profile, then the choice is there to be more adventurous.

Active, passive and holistic

The best way to proceed is to build a holistic investment plan, leaving out the products and managers of investments to begin with. Decide on your investment criteria, the term and availability of your investment and how much risk you can undertake. Then take into account other factors, such as tax status, and the need to save or reduce tax or not, and what personal allowances are available to you. You can then asset allocate your investment portfolio into the main asset classes, defined by your risk profile, and the amount of money available to invest, and taking into account the need for income, capital growth or both, and for how long. You also need to decide whether you are a passive (leaving things to the fund managers) or an active investor (who wishes to be involved at all times in investment decision- making), and what sort of investment structure you require.

If funds are small, then you would probably take the collective funds route, investing into unit trusts, OEICs and investment trusts; whilst larger funds investors (usually over £100,000) would opt for a discretionary fund manager to manage their funds and report back to them. Other considerations would be if you had a lump sum to invest, or whether you wished to make monthly contributions – most savers choose the latter.

Fees and charges

Influencing decisions could include the charges and fees payable to product providers and advisers. Whilst advisers can take commissions at this time on investments and pensions, from 2012 they will not be able to do so and will have to charge you a fee. This does not apply to protection business, such as life policies, where commissions can still be taken.

Because remuneration of the adviser will become more fee driven, expect more justification for investment recommendations. The fee agreed can be paid by the investor or by the product provider acting on the investor's instructions. An average commission would be 3% plus 0.5% ongoing trail commission/fee (although many investors have found to their detriment that some advisers take a lot more), and you will see fees panning out at the same rate, or even reducing. Product charges have also become more transparent over the past few years, as product providers seek to produce a plain vanilla offering and add on charges consistent with client requirement's, and disclosable to them. As the number of well-qualified IFAs decrease in the future (it is expected that up to 20% of current IFAs will leave the industry over the next two years as they and their current businesses cannot cope with new regulations and qualifications that will affect them), the product providers may become more desperate to find distribution for their products, which will become more homogeneous. The main differentiating factors will be price and charges and unusual product sets, and we are already seeing better charging structures for clients coming through now. From 2012 will also be the last of the incentive deals to get investors to buy from certain product providers. These will include higher allocation amounts for investments, which will disappear, as one provider cannot offer any incentive over another. The focus will then be on investment performance, and active investors will not tolerate poor performance with their money. There will be a surge in bank advisers offering their products, and these will take the low to middle ground, and for the non-discerning investor, the high ground.

Epilogue

Conclusions

You will have learned about investments that are tax-free, those that are tax-reducing, those that are taxable, but also efficient because of allowances, and those that defer tax. Throughout there have been full explanations of the different types of investments, and their tax status.

We have learned about investment planning and where it fits into the wider financial planning, and the need to plan for families and also succeeding generations. Also how to relate investments to financial planning, and an understanding of the taxation implications of investments and for investors.

The investment universe is exceptionally large and can be complicated. In this book I have tried to deal with the more common types of investments and where they fit in to the picture.

Included in your planning is the need to do something about it now and to prepare for the next tax year end.

Abbreviations

ADL	Activities of Daily Living
AER	Annual Equivalent Rate – a notional rate that illustrates what the annual rate of interest would be if the interest was compounded each time it was paid. Where interest is paid annually, the quoted rate and the AER are the same.
AIM	Alternative Investment Market
APR	Annual Percentage Rate/ Agricultural property relief
ASP	Alternatively Secured Pension
BPR	Business property relief
CEO	Chief executive Officer
CGT	Capital gains tax
CPI	Consumer price index
CTF	Child Trust Fund
CVS	Corporate Venturing scheme
DGT	Discounted Gift trust
DMO	Debt Management Office
E	Euros
EIS	Enterprise investment scheme
EPA	Enduring Power of Attorney
ETF	Exchange Traded Fund
EZ	Enterprise zone
FSA	Financial Services Authority
FSCS	Financial Services Compensation Scheme
HMRC	Her Majesty's Revenue & Customs
IFAP	IFA Promotions
IHT	Inheritance Tax
ISA	Individual Savings Account
ITA	Income Taxes Act
L & G	Legal and General
LLP	Limited Liability Partnership
LPA	Lasting Power of Attorney
LTA	Lifetime Allowance
MCA	Married Couples Allowance
MIP	Monthly Investment Plan
NEST	National Employers Savings Trust
NRB	Nil Rate Band
NS & I	National Savings and Investments
OEIC	Open-ended investment company
PIBS	Permanent Interest bearing shares
PLA	Purchased life annuity
PRIP	Portfolio Regular Investment Plan

RPI	Retail prices index
SAA	Special Annual Allowance
SDLT	Stamp Duty land tax
SIPP	Self Invested Personal Pension
SSAS	Small Self Administered Scheme
TEP	Traded Endowment Plan
UK	United Kingdom
USP	Unsecured Pension – drawdown funds before age 75
VAT	Value Added tax
VCT	Venture Capital Trust

Bibliography

Tax Insider Newsletters: Tax Portal Ltd, 28 Knightsbridge Court, Palmyra Square, South Warrington, Cheshire, WA1 1TA

Business Protection Simplified by Tony Granger (Management Books 2000)

Inheritance Tax Simplified by Tony Granger (Management Books 2000)

Pensions Simplified by Tony Granger (Management Books 2000)

School and University Fees Simplified by Tony Granger (Management Books 2000)

Core Tax Annuals: Income Tax 2010/11 by Sarah Laing CTA (Bloomsbury Professional)

Core Tax Annuals: Capital Gains Tax 2010/11 by Rebecca Cage et al (Bloomsbury Professional)

Tolley's Tax Guide by Homer, Burrows et al (LexisNexis)

Tolley's Practical Tax Service (LexisNexis)

Personal Financial Planning Manual by RSM Bentley Jennison

HMRC website

DWP website

General Web and internet research, Citywire, Money Marketing, FT, IFA advisers etc.

Provider and Service Provider Listings

Future editions will have provider listings for investors seeking further information.

If a product provider please contact Tony Granger at email tony@tonygranger.com for more information on how to place a directory listing.

Index

For further confidential information on tax-efficient investments and investment planning, or to host a seminar in your area, either email the author at tony@tonygranger.com or send this page to:

Tony Granger
Mentor Professional
11 Melbourne Rise,
Bicton Heath, Shrewsbury
SY3 5DS
Tel: 01743 360827 Fax: 01743 240381
Email: tony@tonygranger.com
www.tonygranger.com

Name _____

Address _____

_____

_____

_____

_____

Postcode _____

Telephone: _____

Fax: _____

Email: _____

Please photocopy this page to avoid spoiling your book